THE HIDDEN GLORY OF THE INNER MAN

BY
H. SARAYDARIAN

THE AQUARIAN EDUCATIONAL GROUP
30188 Mulholland Highway • Agoura, California 91301

© 1968 by H. Saraydarian
1st revised impression, 1975
of *Magnet of Life*
Library Congress Number 74-33110
ISBN 11794-15-8

Printed in the United States of America
Typography by R S Typographics
Printing by George Banta Co., Inc.

CONTENTS

Dedicated To
Djwhal Khul

ABOUT THE AUTHOR

H. Saraydarian was born in Asia Minor. Since his childhood he has tried to understand the mystery called man.

He visited monasteries, ancient temples and mystery schools in order to find the answers to his burning questions.

He lived with sufis, dervishes, Christian mystics and with teachers of occult lore. It took long years of discipline and sacrifice to absorb the Ancient Wisdom from its true sources. Meditation became a part of his daily life, and service a natural expression of his soul.

He lectured in many cities; he wrote numerous articles in various occult, philosophic and religious publications.

He is a violinist, philosopher, teacher, lecturer, mechanical engineer, meteorologist and composer.

The Hidden Glory of the Inner Man reveals the beauty of the real individuality behind the man of flesh and bone.

He explains how a man can meet his real self and release himself from agelong identifications with the body. In very lucid language he speaks about the Transpersonal Self, the Solar Angel, and shows how the inner man can externalize himself through mystic doors found in his electro-magnetic field. He speaks about the seed atoms, meditation, soul-infusion, expansion of awareness and about the steps of self-actualization, illumination, meditation, etc.

Anyone yearning to surpass himself, to enter new dimensions of awareness and to develop a true sense of communication with his fellow man and with the greater cosmos will find this book a must.

Works by H. Saraydarian:

The Inner Blooming
The Great Invocation
The Science of Becoming Oneself
The Science of Meditation
The Fiery Carriage and Drugs
Cosmos in Man
Christ The Avatar of Sacrificial Love
The Bhagavad Gita,
    translated from the original Sanskrit

INTRODUCTION

For those who have experienced something of *soul* within them, which a Tibetan sage calls "a beauty and a power, an active liberating force, a wisdom and a love...", this book will speak to their hearts and will enlighten their understanding of this phenomenon. The author draws upon a wide background in comparative religion, monastic life, and active work in an Oriental-Christian church, and esoteric and occult studies to effect a compelling synthesis of ideas and analogies which reveal the nature of soul-experience and its place in psycho-spiritual maturation. What he says is basically that spiritual essence, that perennial philosophy, which the enlightened sages of all times have taught to their disciples. He does, however, explain some of the more technical aspects of *soul* in ways which can be more readily understood by Occidentals.

There is a new trend in western psychology which is leading towards the insights depicted in this book. This is the humanistic movement with its emphasis on health, self-actualization, creativity, psychosynthesis, and peak experiences. It is hoped that the reader may be able to see the vision portrayed by the author and sense the movement towards a reconciliation between psychological science and the Ancient Wisdom. The author's concepts can be considered Oriental, but they do have an experiential basis, and indicate that there is far more to man than just id, conditioned reflexes, mechanical reactions, or the personality-bound sense of identity.

This book points towards vaster dimensions of mind and being than Occidentals ordinarily dare to dream about. Supporting this view are the findings of western parapsychological research which suggest that there is a factor in man which transcends the material space-time continuum as we currently understand it. In this time of planetary crisis, when the mind of modern man has prolonged the life-span resulting in an imminent danger of over-population and famine, when the release of nuclear energy threatens to annihilate humanity rather than to make deserts bloom, when people view competing ideological abstractions as more important than mankind as a whole, a higher focus than mind is needed, a perspective which can lead man to view himself with greater dignity. It is only when a man feels this dignity of *soul* within him that he can view others as having a right-to-dignity. This is basic to a faith in the heart of mankind which is so needed in our time to overcome the loss of nerve and the despair so prevalent.

The esoteric teaching regarding the *soul* is not a vague, misty yearning for the good, the true, and the beautiful, but is really quite technical and detailed. The author clarifies mainly occult points about Soul, Solar Angel and the Monad which are rather different than the teachings of the numerous metaphysical groups. He explains the principle of sacrifice of the higher for the lower which forms the central position of all esoteric teaching, both technical and in the life of discipleship and initiation (progressive stages of expanding awareness). This concept is the real essence of Christianity as well, only the Christian churches limit it to a specific historic event centered around the life of Jesus. The esoteric tradition, however, has a wider perspective, within the context of a cosmic, trans-humanistic, psycho-spiritual evolution.

Many are mentally prepared to accept such a viewpoint, but are puzzled as to how to achieve results in living. This confusion and searching is reflected in the enormous appeal of psychedelic drugs, the ever-widening influence of Oriental religions in America (especially Zen Buddhism,) and the many meditation-study groups springing up over the entire country. A balanced, integrative and maturity-enhancing path towards soul awareness is described in this book. The possible dangers of psychedelic drugs, hypnotism and efforts to develop psychic faculties prematurely are explained. Of particular appeal, is that this is done in terms of technical, esoteric and occult thought, and not in a moralistic, frightening, authoritarian manner.

It is the author's and my sincere hope that this book will lead many of today's young people to a more mature and knowing understanding of transcendental states of mind and being than is presented to them by the advocates of psychedelic drugs and a variety of personality-centered groups. For all those who suffer needlessly from a restrictive outlook on life, it is our hope that they may find a healing release.

ROBERT CONSTAS, M.D.

The princess was driven out by her father from his palace. She fled into the dark forest, carrying with her as her luggage nothing but three walnut shells. One contained a robe made of the light of the stars, another a robe from the light of the sun, and the third a robe from the light of the moon. Lost in the night, she hid herself in a hollow tree, and being found in the morning by the huntsman of the realm to which she had come, was asked her name and from whence she came. She had forgotten them both. He therefore took her to the castle of the Lord whom he served where she was put to work at the most menial tasks in the scullery, and allowed out only at the time of the great festivals of the year—Christmas, Easter and Mid-summer—when, wearing one of her robes from the light of the celestial bodies, she danced at the ball. There she was seen by the Prince, who admired her, loved her, married her and ultimately carried her back again to the realm from which she had descended.

—FROM A FAIRY TALE

PREFACE

What other knowledge can compare with that which enables us to form a right appreciation of the spiritual potentialities bearing on the permanent and imperishable elements of our being?[1]

—A. P. Sinnett

The path of progress is nothing else but the process of knowing and becoming oneself. It is the path of transmutation.

Upon this path, as man passes through the following stages he feels and thinks:

a. There is nature and I am one with it.
b. I am, I exist as a body.
c. I am emotions, wishes, pleasure.
d. I am body, emotions and mind.
e. I am NOT a body, emotions and a mind.
f. What am I?

In the first stage, he sees nature—the mountains, rivers, forests, seas…he does not feel himself separate from nature, but as a part of it.

In the second stage, the pain, the cold, the heat, hunger, the disorders of his body force him to feel that he exists; he is a body, a separate whole by himself. Here emerges the sensation of an intense fear. He is separated from Mother Nature; his little *boat* floats in the open sea and there is fear behind every wave.

In the third stage, he has learned, somehow, to deal with nature. Fear has trained him, increased the sensitivity of his nerves and made them ready for pleasure and pain. The whole aim of the man now is to feel happy, to have as much pleasure as he can have by every means possible.

In the fourth stage, the fears, pains, and pleasures cultivate the mental powers in him. He feels now that he is not only body, but also emotion and mind. For ages, most of humanity has been living in this stage, creating civilizations and cultures all based upon emotion and feeling.

In the fifth stage, the mind has the controlling position. Man thinks that he is the mind; and the mind tries to solve all the mysterious problems of the emotions, feelings and the psychological processes which are going on continuously within him. Here he reaches the conclusion that he is the mind, lives within the skull, and communicates with the outer world via his nerves or senses….

In the sixth stage, some high inner experiences, some psychological problems, some unexpected revelations, relationships, inspiration, or visions force him to the conclusion that he is not a body; he is not the sum-total of his emotions or pleasures; he is not a mind…but all these are tools of communication, vehicles and instruments, used by an unknown center found in him.

It is here that the process of knowing oneself starts….

In all ages, people who reached this stage have asked the important question—Who am I?

And they have heard continuously the wise words of the Temple of Delphi—

"Man, know thyself and thou wilt know the universe and the Gods."

This book is an endeavor to answer this ageless question.

---

1. A. P. Sinnett, *The Growth of the Soul*, p. 5.

CHAPTER 1

THE TRUE LIGHT

The meaning of the universe is revealed in the soul. The meaning is not to be found in what we see, hear, and touch, but in what the soul brings to light from its own unseen depth.

—Rudolph Steiner

There are many interesting things in life. The term "interest," however, is a relative one, and its meaning changes from one man to another. That which interests me now may not interest me in the future; and again, that which holds no interest for myself and others at the present time may interest all of us later on. We can also say that there are transitory as well as eternal interests; and interests which originate from diversified motives and sources.

We can say further that the things which hold our interest clearly reflect our education, our level of understanding, and our sense of value. There are also areas of interest which as yet do not exist for the majority of people, because they have neither the ability nor the preparation to appreciate them.

Those who have progressed to some degree on the path of realization and sublimation gradually change their fields of interest, as a child outgrows his toys, and dedicates himself to education, culture and service.

But there is one subject around which have revolved, perhaps, all sciences throughout all ages. In the course of human history there has never been a civilization which has not been interested in this subject. The wise man and the peasant; the atomic scientist of today as well as the primitive man of the past all have turned their eyes towards that everlasting subject, each drawing his own conclusion and inspiration from it. This subject, this evergreen flower, is the *Human Soul.*

And why is it so interesting? How can it be otherwise? For the soul is the key to life and death, the root of existence; the source of all virtues and beauties. It is the soul that gives eternal meaning to our loves and sacrifices, and without it all our joys end in the grave.

Those who have thought about the transience of life, those who have met the shadow of death, and those who have seen their loved ones pass from this life have all entertained thoughts of the soul. These thoughts have consoled them or have led them into bitterness, or perhaps changed all their attitudes and relationships, or left them prey to the winds of illusions and vanities.

And who has not thought about the transience of life or the possibility of eternal life, about the generations of the past and present, about the source of genius and wisdom, and about the advanced teachers and leaders of the world?

All these thoughts pass through the gates of the soul. Anyone who can enter the realm of that mystery can solve the problems of life and death, of truth and illusion.

11

The idea of the soul has attracted past generations throughout many ages and for centuries to come will control the interests of future generations.

In the *Upanishads,* a section of the *Brihâdaranyaka Upanishad,* there is a conversation between the king and a wise man called Yâjñavalkya, which runs as follows:

The King says—
"What is the light of man, O Yâjñavalkya?

—O king, answers the wise man, the light of the man is the sun. By the light of the sun man sits down, walks about, performs his work, and returns home.—

—It is even so, O Yâjñavalkya, but when the sun has set, what is then the light of man?

—The moon, O king, is even his light. By the moonlight he sits down, walks about, performs his work, and returns home.—

—It is even so, Yâjñavalkya, but what is the light of man when the sun has set, the moon has set, fire is at rest?

—Speech is even his light. By the light of speech he sits down, walks about, performs his work and returns home. Therefore, O king of kings, at a time when one cannot distinguish his own hand, he resorts there whence speech proceeds.—

—It is even so, Yâjñavalkya, but what is the light of man, when the sun has set, the moon has set, fire is at rest, and speech is at rest?

—O king, the light of man is his soul, his true self. By the light of soul he sits down, walks about, performs his work, and returns home...

—But what is the soul, O Yâjñavalkya?

—It abides in the heart, and uses the organs. It is the inner light, the knower, and it never changes—living in both worlds, thinking and acting. At the time of sleep, it passes beyond this world and beyond all forms of death..."

And the conversation continues in deep beauty and explains the qualities of the soul, the significance of darkness and light, and concludes—

"So the one who recognized the soul, becomes peaceful, serene and satisfied...and sees his real self in the great self, all in One Self, as the self; evil cannot burn him, he burns all evil. Free from evil, free from impurity...He becomes the Great Soul...O king..."

In all civilizations and in all races enlightened men have conducted a search for the soul and have worshipped the soul, thereby amassing great wealth, building countless temples, creating orders, brotherhoods, mysteries, sacred hymns, literature, architecture, and musical masterpieces.

In the Egyptian *Book of the Dead*, which was written three to four thousand years before Christ, we read—

"My soul shall not be fettered to my body at the gates of the grave; but
I shall enter in peace, and I shall come forth in peace."

In this scientific age, has the search for the soul come to an end? We can say
that the quest for the soul has not come to an end; on the contrary, day by day it is
gaining momentum because man throughout all his endeavors is searching for
himself.

In the field of RELIGION a new development is taking place. People are more
tolerant of each other's religions and those who study comparative religions are
discovering that the source of light is one, and the path of light is one. In all
churches people are putting their houses in order and the clergy are gradually
becoming less devotional and more intellectual. In the field of philosophy,
spiritual values are receiving more emphasis. In any large library today, one may
find hundreds of volumes written about Oriental spiritual philosophy; and
Chinese, Indian, Egyptian, and Greek wisdom-literature are now flooding the
world.

In the field of SCIENCE we see a new interest about the energy field of the
human body and about the psychic powers latent in man.

In the field of PSYCHOLOGY we see a new break through toward the transpersonal self toward experiences registered with higher senses.

In the field of ART there is a new tendency to use it to reveal beauty and
meanings in the universe and the Cosmos. Many artists today through many forms
of their arts are trying to give birth to the future man.

People are feeling that there is a greater destiny for each man and for all
humanity as a whole and they are no longer satisfied with what our materialistic
civilization provided them.

The Soul is the door leading to Group-consciousness, to universality, to the
one unified whole, and toward global humanity. Our children are naturally
oriented to these concepts, everywhere in the world, the new-age is dawning.

CHAPTER 2

THE LOCATION OF THE SOUL

Behold, the Kingdom of God is within you.

—St. Luke 17:21

A. A. Bailey's book, *The Soul and its Mechanism* mentions certain authorities who have been especially interested in the problem of the soul and have given important ideas about its location.

"Dr. Richard Muller-Freinfels says, 'To write the history of man's belief in soul one would have at the same time to write the history of the whole human race.' " (p. 72)

"Plato held that the vital principle was in the brain and that the brain and spinal cord were coordinators of vital force." (p. 85)

"Strato placed it in the forepart of the brain, between the eyebrows."

"Hippocrates placed the consciousness or soul in the brain."

"Herophilus made the calamus scriptorius[1] the chief seat of the soul."

"Erasistratos located the soul in the cerebellum, or the little brain, and stated that it was concerned in the coordination of movement."

"Galen, the great forerunner of modern medical methods, argued for the fourth ventricle of the brain as the home of the soul in man."

"Hippolytus (3rd century A.D.) says, 'The membranes in the head are gently moved by the spirit which advances toward the pineal gland. Near this is situated the entrance to the cerebellum, which admits the current of spirit and distributes it into the spinal column. This cerebellum by an ineffable and inscrutable process, attracts through the pineal gland the spiritual and life giving substance.' " (p. 86)

"St. Augustine regarded the soul as located in the middle ventricle."

"The Arabian philosophers, who so strongly moulded thought in the Middle Ages, identified the ventricles of the brain as the seat of the soul or conscious life."

"Roger Bacon regarded the center of the brain as the place where the soul could be found." (p. 87)

"Ludovicus Vives regarded the soul as the principle, not only of conscious life, but of life in general; the heart is the center of its vital or vegetative activity, the brain of its intellectual activity."

"Mundinus, a famous anatomist of the Middle Ages, believed firmly in 'animal spirits.' He thought that these animal spirits passed into the third ventricle by a narrow passage. He also thought that the cellules of the brain are the seat of the intellect."

"Vesalius, the first to discern the differences between the gray and white

---

1. The point at the base of the brain where the posterior columns of the medulla oblongata diverge, leaving them the space known as the 4th ventricle named from the likeness to a writing pen; Funk & Wagnalls New Standard Dictionary.

matter of the brain and to describe the five ventricles, distinguished three souls, and assigned the brain the chief soul, the sum of the animal spirits, whose functions were distinctly mental."

"Servious located the soul in the Aqueduct of Sylvius, the channel connecting the third and fourth ventricle of the brain."

"Telesio thought that the soul was the subtlest form of matter, a very delicate substance, enclosed within the nervous system and therefore eluding our senses. Its seat is chiefly the brain, but it extends also to the spinal cord, the nerves, arteries, veins, and the covering membranes of the internal organs. He assumed, beside the material soul in man, a divine non-corporeal soul directly implanted by God, which united with the material soul." (p. 88)

Will Durant in his *Mansions of Philosophy* says:

> "The life is not a function of the force, the form is a product of the Life: the weight and solidity of matter are the result and expressions of intra-atomic energy, and every muscle or nerve in the body is moulded expression of desire."

Present-day science is abandoning its former ideas about matter and is slanting towards the plane of abstract thinking, of the invisible, of the unrevealed.

Science claims matter does not exist. As we see it, matter is energy or motion itself. Science also teaches that the most compact condensation is the absolute vacuum, the static. However, it cannot yet tell us what energy is, what motion is, what space is, what vacuum is and what absolute static is. It cannot tell us because it does not have enough "sense-organs" to come in contact with the finer energies and to register them. We know, however, that in the future science will reveal to us the spiritual world; it conquered Everest and will conquer also space and time. And one day it will show us our essential nature behind the form.

The professor of Astronomy at the University of Glasgow, W. M. Smarts, in *The Origin of the Earth* says:

> "When we study the universe and appreciate its grandeur and orderliness, it seems to me that we are led to the recognition of a Creative Power and Cosmic purpose that transcends all that our limited minds can comprehend."

Some of our present-day thinkers hold that beyond matter, space and energy there exists a mysterious "Electricity" which we call *Life*. This life is conscious and has a plan or purpose as the manifested universe; and all its laws are founded upon an immeasurable consciousness—a mind—that is everywhere and in everything, as the creator of urges and purposeful actions. Within that great Life, there are individual lives. Life is everywhere, and everything is an expression of Life. Those individual lives who focus and use the energy, space, time and matter found in Cosmos, *are human beings.*

Some scientists tell us that there is only one mind from which everything emanates. Hence, everything is condensed mind and, as such, has the potentiality to grow, to become spiritualized and to have will and direction of its own. Sir James Jeans, says:

"The Universe gradually begins to look more like a great thought than like a great machine. Mind no longer appears as an accidental intruder into the realm of matter; we are beginning to suspect that we ought rather to hail it as the Creator and Governor of the realm of matter, not of course, our individual minds, but the mind in which the atoms, out of which our individual minds have grown, exist as thoughts."[2]

People once believed that it was the grey matter of the brain which was utilized in the thinking process. Later, it was believed that the character of a man and his qualities were the results of the glands. Still later, the grey matter of the brain and the ductless glands were thought to be the essential causes of the intelligence and behavior of man. However, subsequent psychological research proved that the grey matter of the brain and the ductless glands were the result and effect of certain inner causes of the existence of which the scientists were not aware.

In the Ancient Wisdom, the Soul was known as a "Son of Mind." Certain scientists maintained that the whole universe is the result of a mind which thinks and, in thinking, produces these manifestations. In the Ancient *Upanishads*, we find the following words: "The One Being meditated, and the worlds manifested." Some scientists hold that the mind builds the brain, as its vehicle of manifestation, to enable it to evolve and cultivate closer relationships with the outer world. Others claim that there are sources of light in man which transcend the mind as, for example, the intuition. Dr. Alexis Carrel in his famous book *Man, the Unknown* says:

"Obviously, great discoveries are not the product of intelligence alone. Men of genius, in addition to their powers of observation and comprehension, possess other qualities such as intuition and creative imagination. Through intuition they learn things ignored by other men, perceive relations between seemingly isolated phenomena and they unconsciously feel the presence of the unknown treasure. All great men are endowed with intuition. They know, without analysis, without reasoning, what is important for them to know. The great man, or the simple whose heart is pure, can be led by it to the summits of mental and spiritual life." (p. 120)

On another page, referring to mind, he says:

"The mind is hidden within the living matter, completely neglected by physiologists and economists, almost unnoticed by physicians; and yet it is the most colossal power of the world." (p. 116)

Again, we read in the teachings of wisdom:

"When the intuition functions in any human being, he is enabled to take direct and correct action, for he is in touch with the Plan, with pure and unadulterated fact and undistorted ideas, free from illusion, and coming directly from the Divine or Universal Mind." (A. A. Bailey)

---

2. Sir James Jeans, *The Mysterious Universe*, Macmillan 1930, pp. 157-158.

"The intuition is the energy of wisdom. This wisdom energy is the only type of force which is adequate to dispel the miasmas, the fogs and mists of the world of glamour." (A. A. Bailey)

The same author in *Cosmic Fire* says:

"The mind may be defined as the intelligent will and ordered purpose of every self-conscious entity."

Thus the representatives of many fields of science approach the revelations given ages ago. A revelation is different from knowledge gained through experience. A revelation is a treasure hitherto hidden, which is handed to humanity. Humanity sees that treasure, becomes aware of its awesome beauty and possibilities, but can neither use it immediately nor explain it. As the ages pass, man gradually discovers the means to absorb and use it, and through it cultivates the ability to understand new revelations. A revelation is a vision, a purpose and a plan. Everything already exists, but only reveals itself to us when we are awakened spiritually, mentally and morally. Revelations are pure ideas, existing on the plane of intuition. People who have cultivated their minds and possess the power of intuition can reach inward and bring forth revelations. In revelation one recognizes a new truth and understands its source.

The link between the worlds of intuition and mind is the Soul. The Soul itself is a revelation, and it is a unit of energy which reveals the hidden path to innermost worlds.

CHAPTER 3

THE ANGEL
The Transpersonal Self

For I say unto you, that in heaven their angels do always behold the face of my Father which is in heaven.

—Matt. 18:10

In Oriental traditions we are told that man has a guiding or protecting angel. Our grandmothers used to tell us that "our angel would be angry if we lived a life not in harmony with him," and also that he can leave us, or "separate himself from us."

In the Psalms King David says, "Cast me not away from thy presence, and take not thy holy spirit from me." Behind these simple words exists a deep truth. The Ancient Wisdom tells us that the real man is not his Soul. The man is not a Soul but has a Soul. The Soul is the first master of man; lives in man; and leads him toward the light, toward the divine love and toward the divine will. Until man reaches a certain degree of development, the Soul remains with him and guides him; when he reaches this goal the Soul leaves him.

In the New Testament it is written, "The kingdom of God is like leaven, which a woman took and hid in three measures of meal, till the whole was leavened." The masters of the Ancient Wisdom tell us that the three measures refer to the three aspects of personality; physical, emotional and mental. The leaven is the principle of mind which the Soul, the woman, hides in the personality, to leaven it.

In ancient Greek Mythology we also read that Prometheus stole *fire* from the Gods and gave it to man. Prometheus gave man the spark of mind, thus opening for him a way of sublimation, achievement and endless illumination.

In the course of the evolution of man there came a period when the mental spark began to vibrate in his brain and he became more sensitive to subjective influences. In the Ancient Wisdom this critical moment is wonderfully depicted. We are told that the phenomenon called man, throughout eons of time, was growing and living a happy life as in paradise but did not yet have in him the light of self-consciousness or self-recognition or discrimination. He was as a happy baby on his mother's bosom.

Within him there were two shores. On one were the body, the emotions and the instinctive mind; on the other, far away, was the original picture from which he was "created." The bridge between these two shores was missing. Only by crossing this bridge could man reach his divine source, his divine essence, and could the essence approach him for divine transmutation.

He was a shadow, living through the life-current coming from the spark and by the primitive mind principle present in the substance itself. In the ancient days many millions of years ago angels, having lived in previous cycles and on other planets, came to man and sparked in him the principle of mind. These angels, or advanced Souls, were called the Sons of Mind. They put the divine leaven, or the principle of mind-fire, in the three measures of meal which created an atmosphere composed of a rare substance within and around the physical man. Man became the divine spark possessing a form and mental fire given to him by the *Sons of Mind.* However, this was not enough, for man had to pass through even higher developments before reaching perfection. Long ages passed and there came a period in which certain entities called "Solar Angels" incarnated in those who were ready, locating themselves in the substance given to man by the Sons of Mind. In ancient writings this is called the crisis of individualization. Man came to know the difference between "good and evil" and "felt his nudity"; he became conscious of himself; and the long journey to his Father's Home began. How deep and beautiful is the parable of the Prodigal Son who left his father and went away to live his own life. After much suffering, he came to himself and said, "I will arise and go to my father,..." which he did. The father seeing him, said, "My son was lost, and is found." The lost one was the reflection, or the portion of the Father in the three worlds (physical, emotional and mental). The reflection went to its original source, to the Father and he "was found."

According to this, man is a spark of spirit, has a Soul or Angel, and a lower self which we call personality. The two shores of man were bridged and, "by the approximation of these two poles, light is produced, a flame shineth forth, sphere of radiant glory is seen which gradually increases the intensity of its light, its heat and its radiance until its capacity is reached, or that which we call perfection."

Mind is a substance, a very sensitive and subtle substance, but it is not the thinker. The thinker is the Soul of man. Through long ages the Soul holds itself as a latent central energy, but can only control the personality at first during dark, critical times; however, its presence helps develop the mental body and, through it, the Soul gradually controls the man and the physical world. Those people who, from ancient times, were able to sense the presence of the Soul and live life according to its rules, were the Initiates who brought light to men and increased the light of humanity.

The presence of the Soul created complicated problems for man in the early days of his evolution, especially in times of crisis when he felt a duality within himself.

Modern psychology has vaguely described the duality of man. It has noted also that sometimes man is not a whole but a composite made up of many parts. Sometimes he is the lower self—the body, emotions, and mental states—and sometimes he is a point of beauty, sublimated and divine. Often there occurs a conflict within man between his higher and lower levels, and sometimes there are two or more motivating powers working within him at the same time.

The primary purpose of man is to bring about an integration and unity among the three lower aspects, then between personality and Soul, and eventually between the Soul-infused Personality and the Monadic Spark. The term personality refers to the sum total of man's physical, emotional and mental vehicles and forces. It is with these vehicles that the unfolding, developing human soul is identified and controlled for ages.

These three vehicles are the *persona* of the unfolding, developing human soul who gradually organizes them, integrates them, and uses them to achieve his goals. Thus within the three vehicles, the real Personality is the unfolding human soul, the "lost" spark of God. When the unfolding human soul integrates his vehicles, another great step is revealed to him. This is the process of Soul infusion. In this process the Personality, or the unfolding human soul makes a contact with the Transpersonal Self, the Solar Angel, and eventually after conflicts of many centuries, he fuses himself with that great Guide. (See chapter 16)[1]

The third step is to bring the Soul-infused Personality to the realization that, he is the divine spark, the Monad. This is the major test of the Transpersonal Self in regard to man. When this stage has been reached the Solar Angel has completed its age-long duty and stands aside. The man has become a Soul.

Duality expresses itself differently on each plane. Man starts to progress when he gradually conquers duality and achieves integration with his higher Self. Hence the process of sublimation in which the lower obeys the higher, the "individual integrates himself into the Whole." For example, two opposing urges may emerge on any of our planes. They can destroy a man if they continue to battle each other without reaching a "conclusion," or they can sublimate him if by a transmutative process, the lower, the material, begins to obey or harmonize with the higher, the ideal. The transmutation process leads to the development of the Voice of conscience and to renunciations, spiritual conversions and great sacrifices. When the higher aspect of the conflicting pair of opposites in the inner world of man gains victory over the lower, you have a new man—a new-born man—relatively free from the lower activities or tendencies.

As a man cannot start to live his own life until separated from the womb of his mother, neither can he enter into the way of real progress until he senses the existence of duality within himself. Gradually moving onto the higher levels of duality, one day he consciously realizes that in him there are two poles separated by a middle point, the point of equilibrium. In him is the pole of matter and the pole of the Divine Spark or spirit, separated by the eternal bridge or Soul which expresses itself as the intellect of man through his mental substance. Hence there are the urges of the material pole and the urges of the spiritual pole and, between them, the principle of understanding or sublimation. Since man has become capable of creating an equilibrium between these two opposite points and their urges, he can become a triangle and thereby a unity. Unity cannot be achieved until a point of balance between the two poles has been established. All mental, psychological and physical ills of the world or of man result from inner conflicts between the higher and lower. The secret of health, joy and success is harmony, integration and sublimation.

Perhaps you have seen someone who, coming out of his house, takes a few steps and then turns back, stops in a pensive, uncertain manner then continues on his way; a moment later, he again turns back, takes a few more steps, stops, and eventually continues on his way. This is the outer expression of the inner struggle of a man who is the victim of two conflicting energies, emotions or thoughts. From such conflicts come dullness of mind, nervous breakdowns, hopelessness, vacillation in self-determination, lack of courage, and perhaps mental diseases with their countless effects.

1. Read *Cosmos in Man,* pp. 40, 47-48, 75-79, 191-193.

The existence of two opposing energies can be offset by a third one, a conclusion. However, if this conclusion is on *behalf* of the lower plane the Solar Angel will once again stimulate the man and give him another opportunity to develop new attitudes, new values and higher principles. The lower equilibrium will again be destroyed. This new stimulation may be delayed and the man may enjoy the pleasures of a lower life and robust health for a while longer. *But the Solar Angel never sleeps, and throughout the centuries will carry on its task of sublimation,* just as in the history of humanity Providence sends the Great Ones to revive mankind.

As the descent was gradual, so will the ascent be. Each step has its counterpart. It is possible to establish a state of equilibrium anywhere between these stages, but the secret of ascension is based upon the following: we must constantly strive to destroy a lower equilibrium, or state of interest, and establish a higher equilibrium leading towards greater awareness. The transition from one step to another is called the moment of crisis during which man either falls down or ascends. If he ascends, he gradually forgets the old values and rises to new and more inclusive heights. Behind this conflict lies the duality in man, the two selves in him who, through different forms and by different techniques carry on the conflict upon the battlefield called "man."

CHAPTER 4

THE KNOWER WITHIN US

For now we see through a glass, darkly; but then face to face...

The Solar Angel, or the Soul, is anchored in the pineal gland and uses it as a station of communication with the mechanism called man. The Soul is not enslaved in man and is not handicapped by his physical, emotional and mental limitations. The Soul, being free from time and space, has its own independent life—its own path of development and progress and its own way of service.

It is the Soul that knows, thinks and creates; and conveys to the mind new ideas, inspiration and revelations. The Soul has a twofold function: one for itself, the other for man. Man develops his higher senses to the degree that his soul consciousness unfolds and enters into the light of the Soul. Gradually he builds a better line of communication with his Soul, progressively tapping Its knowledge, age-long experiences, and wisdom.

Generally man on the physical plane knows nothing about the functions of his Soul until he has reached a certain degree of unfoldment and consciously comes in contact with It. Then the knowledge of the Soul becomes his, the eye of the Soul is his, and he passes from the realm of men to the kingdom of Souls. At this stage he starts to have deeper experiences not known to our five senses, and all life for him changes to a process of becoming.

Many people believe that life is a process of giving and taking, and this concept prevents their becoming conscious of their Solar Angels. Man is searching for himself or for the inner source of knowledge, for the center of inner guidance, for the fountain of inspiration. This is the Higher Self which should control all his relationships. Many people place too high a value on their material side and lose the vision of the Higher Self. We can ask with Ouspensky, "which part is bigger in man, the measurable or the unmeasurable?" Of course, the unmeasurable.

Most people today, especially those who have received higher education, put their lives' emphasis upon material objects, and the gratification of their bodies and have a tendency to overlook deeper experiences which cannot be proven by science. The true meaning of science, however, is but the result of experience. A true impression, an intuition, is an experience; it is valid. Man achieves awareness in a different sense and knows that which he has not learned through his five senses or instruments.

Scientific facts are those which we experience through our five senses or instruments. But there are facts which cannot be seen through the microscope or telescope nor perceived by our five senses. These facts are not measurable but we can experience them through our subtle or higher senses. Some of these are: telepathic communications, intuitive understanding, certain dreams, impressions, premonitions and many mystical and religious experiences. Can we consider them unreliable phenomena?

A mother, quite happy one moment, suddenly begins to cry and is overcome by a feeling that her son is dead; she later finds out that he died in battle at the very moment of her grief. Others can foresee events before they occur. Still others receive waves of impressions of high creativity, leadership, etc. Can we label these experiences superstitious or unreliable?

Truly all genuine religious and psychic experiences are factual when they are perceived by people who have highly-developed senses. The people who experience on higher levels are more advanced than most of us and, because we cannot approach these levels, we reject the truth of their experiences, like the man who rejects the discoveries of Mount Palomar because he can see only what is revealed by a toy telescope.

The mind of man is merely a spoon which he is filling from the Ocean of Knowledge, and our knowledge is just a drop from the Ocean of real knowledge, as the knower within us is but an atom of the One who is Omniscient. *In reality the process of learning is a process of becoming what we essentially are.*

When there is an object about which we want to know more we begin to study it. But first we must realize that there is a Knower Who created it and a knower who is trying to gain knowledge of it, and these two knowers stem from the same root. It is not enough to know an object by our five senses for that is to know only its outer form, and the Ancient Wisdom states that every object has a sevenfold existence. There exists an infinity which is different from finiteness and we try to explain infinity in terms of finiteness. Our explanations will appear to us as truth since we are living as finite entities; but once we start to become eternal and infinite, all our former measures will become obsolete. A time will come when we will express ourselves as both finite and eternal. Only on this level—the Soul level—can we expect to know objects as they essentially are. In the process of knowing, knowledge changes into realization and from that state knowing is equal to becoming…*knowing means to be.*

Ouspensky says:

"All the rest was imagination. The real world was a 'world without forms.' The question as to how to fix this state arose continually and I put it to myself many times when I was in the state in which I could receive answers to my questions; but I could never get a direct answer to it, that is, the answer which I wanted. Usually the answer began far away and, gradually widening, included everything so that finally the answer to the question included the answers to all possible questions…many times, perhaps always, I had the feeling that when I passed the second threshold, I came into contact with myself, with the self which was *always within me,* which always saw me and always told me something that I could not understand and could not even hear in an ordinary state of consciousness. The being to whom this voice belonged knew everything, understood everything, and above all was free from thousands of small and distracting 'personal' thoughts and moods. He could take everything calmly, could take everything objectively as it was in reality. And at the same time, *this was I.* How this could be so and why in the ordinary state I was so far from myself, if this was I—that I could not explain."[1]

---

1. P. D. Ouspensky, *A New Model of the Universe,* pp. 321-325.

At times the Solar Angel takes control of the personality and speaks, sings, or writes through him. Its voice is different from the voice of the personality for It has depth and sweetness, and is very impressive. This voice is magnetic and effective and is heard when there is a *need*—a group, national, or universal *need*—or when there is an opportunity to give much-needed rare advice, energy or leadership. A simple man may suddenly become a hero and lead armies; or, with his speech and song, inspire multitudes to achieve a new level of understanding.

In esoteric literature the state in which the consciousness of man functions in the light of his Soul is called the awakened state of consciousness. The state in which man is the victim of his lower self, his glamours and illusions, is called sleep; or the state of ignorance and darkness. In olden days a man was called ignorant if he had no experience of communication with his Soul and existed within the limits of his five senses. Knowledge comes from within, and a man becomes a true knower when his mind is infused with the light of his Soul. Only then does he begin to realize the depth of his former ignorance, and start to use all his new knowledge to work out the Great Plan behind the manifested life.

Only Soul-knowledge can lead us towards happiness, joy and bliss, the state of being our true Selves. The great Sankaracharya says: "There is no higher cause of joy than silence where no mind pictures dwell; it belongs to him who has understood the Self's own being; who is full of the essence of the bliss of the Self."[2]

In occult and esoteric books, in Psychology and Philosophy, there is a great confusion about the nature of the human soul.

The Tibetan Master gave us some clues about this problem in His various books. For example in the *Treatise on White Magic* He says:

A) "At first the soul exerts but little pressure upon these bodies.
B) It identifies itself with the bodies for a long time.
C) Later the soul awakens to the need to dominate its vehicles.
D) Then the soul begins to reorganize, re-orient and rebuild the bodies.
E) Eventually the soul becomes the positive controlling factor."[3]

This is the human soul—the real man, apart of his physical, emotional and mental bodies.

In modern psychology this is called the evolving self, or the evolving human consciousness.

The Solar Angel, which is referred in many esoteric books as the Soul, is not the man, is not the evolving human consciousness, or the evolving self, but the inner Master, the transpersonal Self, whose duty is to guide the evolving human soul into his essence or to the realization of his true nature.

When we speak about the Monad we refer to the essence of the unfolding human soul. The unfolding human soul is the Monad, but identified with physical, emotional and mental worlds. The duty of the Guide, the Solar Angel, or transpersonal Self is to lead the "man" through these three "halls of learning," as they are called, to the "hall of wisdom," to higher planes, where he will reach to the realization of his true Self—the Monad, or in terms of modern psychology—the Transcendental Self.

---

2. Sankaracharya, *The Crest Jewel of Wisdom*, verse 527.
3. Alice A. Bailey, *A Treatise on White Magic*, p. 202.

CHAPTER 5

EXTERNALIZATION

Before thou canst approach the foremost gate thou has to learn to part thy body from thy mind, to dissipate the shadow, and to live in the eternal. For this, thou has to live and breathe in all, as all that thou perceivest breathes in thee; to feel thyself abiding in all things, all things in SELF.[1]

—H. P. B.

There are four exits by which man can withdraw from his body. In the Ancient Wisdom, we are told that there are three doors in the subtle body through which man can exteriorize himself; there is a door near the solar plexus, another near the heart, and a third at the top of the head. These doors may be used according to the achievement of man.

The first form of exteriorization is death, at which time man draws himself out of his body, away from its magnetic field.

Second, man may withdraw himself at the time of a great crisis, danger or fear in which case the withdrawal may be either partial or complete. If the withdrawal is partial, it creates glandular and nervous effects and can destroy some parts of the brain and affect the consciousness adversely. Its slight effects may be seen in people whose state of mind is diffused, uncertain, and without much purpose.

Third, by the use of drugs man sometimes leaves his body and here anaesthetics play an important role.

Fourth, through the advanced technique of meditation and contemplation man can withdraw himself from the body gradually and in a very natural way. Self-hypnosis is a branch of this technique but this creates many problems and does not afford any spiritual usefulness.

In hypnosis the unit of awareness steps out from the sphere of the body through the solar plexus, and enters into the lower strata of the astral world.

In conscious withdrawal the awareness unit steps out through the heart center or through the head center, in both cases the awareness unit, the unfolding human soul remembers his experiences in the subtle worlds. As he withdraws from his body, a tiny thread of light extends from the heart center to the awareness unit. This is called the life thread. When it is cut the body passes away. It is possible that with this thread two other threads extend between the head and the awareness unit, through which all experiences of the unfolding human soul pass to the etheric and dense brain. This is how man remembers his dreams, or experiences in the higher astral, mental or even intuitional planes.

These threads are called the consciousness thread and the antahkarana, one extends from the Soul to the brain, the other extends from the mental unit to the mental permanent atom, to the intuitional and atmic planes.

---

1. H. P. Blavatsky, *The Voice of the Silence,* p. 54.

At the time a man is unconscious through any kind of shock, death or sleep, it is the thread of consciousness, or the thread of the Transpersonal Self that is withdrawn, and man, if not evolved will not remember his "out of body" experiences.

At the time of conscious withdrawal the thread, built by the human soul, the antahkarana, is anchored in the etheric and dense physical brain. It bridges the mental unit and manasic permanent atoms and conveys to the etheric and dense brain all experiences that the human soul is passing through.[2] Thus man remembers all his experiences, and his participation in subjective events taking place upon subtle levels of human existence.

The important thing is to remember that this second thread is the result of striving, service and conscious evolution of the human soul. If he does not build this second thread, he does not have it, and any time he is out of the body, he is unconscious of higher mental and intuitional world experiences. It is possible that a Master of Wisdom can connect His thread to the brain and to the awareness unit of a person and let him remember his out of the body experiences and relations. This is done seldom if such an experience of the person will be of great help to the group, nation or humanity in a critical time, or if he karmically deserves it.

In Egypt, these mysteries were enacted primarily in the Great Pyramid which was designed for this purpose. The same lessons were taught in India and Greece, and in the secret brotherhoods of Asia and South America.[3]

We are told that "among the few foreigners who were permitted to receive this Egyptian initiation were: Plato, Pythagoras, Thales, Lycurgus, Solon, Iamblichus, Plutarch and Herodotus."

Plutarch says:

"At the moment of death, the soul experiences the same impressions as those who are *initiated into the great mysteries.*"

Plato says:

"In consequence of this divine initiation, we become spectators of single and blessed visions, resident in a pure life and were ourselves made immaculate and liberated from this surrounding garment which we call the body and to which we are not bound like an oyster to its shell."[4]

To ancient Egyptians, the grain of wheat was sacred because it was the symbol of the *soul;* they put grains of wheat in the tombs of dead persons, representing the immortality of the soul. Jesus referred to this when He said—"Verily, verily I say unto you, except a grain of wheat fall into the ground and die, it abides alone, but if it die, it bringeth forth much fruit."

"In the Eleusinian Mysteries, every candidate for Initiation in a particular procession carried a grain of wheat in a tiny earthenware bowl. The secret was in the idea that man could die simply as a grain and could rise again into another life."

This is the human soul, who was fallen into the earth, into the threefold man and is going through a mystical death, being identified with the "earth." But

---

2. Read *The Science of Becoming Oneself* by H. Saraydarian, chap. 18.

3. There are interesting experiences given by Paul Brunton in *A Search in Secret Egypt,* pp. 69-72, and by Andrija Puharich in *The Sacred Mushroom,* pp. 20-21, 59-62.

4. Paul Brunton, *A Search in Secret Egypt,* p. 74.

it is here that all his future blooming takes root and as he conquers it, and learns his lessons, he shines with all his beauty that was latent in the seed.

Within the sphere of personality there exists the human-soul, the initial spark, plus the guiding, transpersonal Self—or the Solar Angel. But often other entities may penetrate into this sphere and occupy the mechanism. Such a case is referred in the New Testament, for example:

"They brought to Jesus a dumb man possessed with a devil, and when the devil was cast out, the dumb man spoke and the multitudes marvelled..." Similar cases are recorded in esoteric psychology. There are numerous instances where some "spirits" or "souls" take up residence in the subtle atmosphere of man and cause him many troubles. Today these are no longer mysteries, but are the subject of scientific research. Any man with due preparation can gradually leave his body and look down on his body.

Dr. Brunton as a mature, intellectual man very clearly explains his experience in the following paragraph of his book:

"I noted a trail of faint silvery light projecting itself down from me, the new me, to the cataleptic creature who lay upon the block. This was surprising, but more surprising still was my discovery that this mysterious psychic umbilical cord was contributing towards the illumination of the corner of the King's Chamber where I hovered; showing up the wall stones in a soft moonbeam-like light."[5]

Cases are recorded in which an expert in hypnotism can separate himself from his body for a long time, leaving his body lying on the ground. Generally, in the case of hypnotism or hypnotic trance, the awareness unit in man, separated from the body, cannot communicate with his brain-mind and therefore the subject is in a state of unconsciousness. But upon reaching higher stages of development, a person can consciously leave his body and can register all his experiences while he remains outside his body.

---

5. *Ibid.*

CHAPTER 6

THE INNER GUIDE MAY LEAVE

In some cases...the Solar Angel withdraws and sheds no light upon the prob-lems of man. His purpose in so doing is to give man the opportunity to help himself...[1]

According to the Ancient Wisdom,
—a man can be born without Solar Angel.
—the Solar Angel, after living for some years, may separate itself from the man.

In the first case, the intellect does not develop and the subject remains as mentally retarded. The pineal gland of such a person generally remains unde-veloped and we are told that for this reason they remain as babies; but the Ancient Wisdom teaches us that their glands do not work properly because their Souls remain inactive.

Some people can look into a person's eyes and recognize whether the Soul is absent or partially withdrawn. If It has left the body, the eyes of the subject are like those of a man who is suddenly awakened and not yet fully conscious, appearing empty and dead. If the Soul is partially withdrawn, the eyes express fear, uncertain-ty, and nervousness.

I made a special study of a young man who was about nineteen or twenty years old, and who had the mind of a child of about two or three years of age. His instincts and passions were awake; he was like an animal. After many psychological tests, I was sure that he did not have an "Angel"—he was unable to imagine or to reason and could only repeat whatever he heard without understanding the meaning of the words.

It sometimes happens that the Angel is present but the mechanism is so out-of-order that the Angel cannot express Itself through the body; he remains in a suspended state for a while and eventually departs. Or the Solar Angel may leave the man because of his vices. This situation is explained in *The Secret Doctrine* (vol. III, p. 527) which says:

"There is however, still hope for a person who has lost his Higher Soul through his vices, while he is yet in the body. He may be still redeemed and made to turn on his material nature. For either an intense feeling of repentance or one single earnest appeal to the Ego that has fled, or best of all, an active effort to amend one's ways, may bring the Higher Ego back again." In this case the Thread of connection has not been completely severed.

Sometimes the mind can be blinded by materialistic ambitions and selfish thoughtforms, which create a fog or wall between the Soul and man, separating the man from the Real Thinker. The man can only reflect the thoughtforms in space created by other minds. Such people are easily affected by demagogues and may

---

1. H. Saraydarian, *Cosmos in Man*, p. 49.

easily be led especially in destructive directions.

A Tibetan Sage says that:

"When mind becomes unduly developed, and ceases to unite the higher and the lower, it forms a sphere of its own. This is the greatest disaster that can overtake the human unit."[2]

We must not forget that though the Soul is the inner light It can be used for selfish and material purposes. When used incorrectly, a fog or wall is gradually created which prevents communication between the mental body, the mind and the Soul, and in due time man finds himself the victim of contradictory ideas and actions. Such people may attempt suicide or become mentally unbalanced because life has lost its purpose, its plan, and they can see no hope for the future.

"Entities" that take possession of the minds of living people are not Solar Angels nor Souls, but "spirits" as they are sometimes called. These entities are usually the "souls" of low-grade men who have passed away and entirely enveloped by low-grade thoughts and emotions, feel a strong craving for earth life. They may approach people who are magnetically in tune with them, occupy their bodies and force the subjects to partake of intense sexual activities, to use drugs and alcohol, and even to commit crimes. The possessed ones may literally hear voices suggesting behavior that is against their better judgment. Unfortunately, they often obey the voices. (I am not referring to the "voices" that one may hear from his subconscious mind or from his reactive mind, but, voices coming from "entities"). There are many such people in mental institutions whom modern physicians are unable to help; they can only record the cases. These patients provide the channel of entry for the entities by their own emotional conflicts, resentments, past relations, and obstructed sexual and aggressive energies. People of great spiritual achievement by their strong and purifying vibrations, can help possessed victims and cast such entities out of their energy fields.

All creation is an act of sacrifice and sometimes in occult books the Souls are called the Sons of Sacrifice. It seems to me that the best way to approach our Souls and *become a Soul* is the way of sacrifice. Our sacrifices are the measure of our achievements and achievement means to be close to the source of our being. Our inner being is a drop of sacrifice as our God is fire and sacrifice. Whenever there is sacrifice, there is God, there is Life.

Who can sacrifice? One who is more spirit than matter, one who is more inclusive and less separative, one who knows from practical experience that *there is no other.* Sacrifice does not mean doing a favor for somebody or slowing down so that another may go faster. It means living as closely as possible to our inner Guide. Sacrifice means expressing the God-Life in steady radiation of Light, Love, Harmlessness and divine will. It means transmutation. Only through transmutation can we transcend our limitations and earn the right to live as Souls, full of beauty and glory.

2. A. A. Bailey, *Cosmic Fire,* p. 261.

CHAPTER 7

THE SELF

Remember yourself always and everywhere.

—G. Gurdjieff

The reader will note that man resembles a triangle, one point representing the world of the personality (physical, emotional and mental), the second point representing the Soul, and the upper one symbolizing the Spark of life. The Soul, as has been said, is a separate being—the inner Master, "the Hope of Glory" Who leads us towards light, love and sacrifice.

The personality is the sum-total of our physical, emotional and mental states. The Spark of light is the *Real Man,* the Individuality who is an imperishable, invulnerable portion of God and a drop of bliss which, in occult literature, is called "the Father." The man, in his essence, is a divine Spark, reflected upon the three worlds of personality, and it is this reflection which we call the "lower self," or the unfolding human soul.

"The Lord is Spirit, and where the Spirit of the Lord is, there is liberty; but we all, with open faces beholding as in *a glass* the Glory of the Lord, are changed into the same image from glory to glory as by the spirit of the Lord."[1] This is the real teaching of the Self. Again, the same truth is found in the Ancient Wisdom, "The spiritual spark beholding his image on the waves of space (physical, emotional and mental bodies)—is whispering—'this is I.' "

The myth of *Narcissus* refers to the above fact. We are told that "Narcissus was a youth of great beauty who fell in love with his own image reflected in the water and was therefore changed into a flower and bound to the earth." The divine spark is the Self plus the plane with which it identifies itself. It becomes the reflection of Itself in the lower bodies.

When the real man identifies with his physical body and lives as a body and for the body—that is his self. When the man develops himself and enters the world of emotions, lives there, and becomes a man fused with his emotions and feelings—that is his self. If he ascends further, and lives as a mentally-oriented man, or as a mind, and sees the difference between his body and emotions and "himself"—then his self is his mental world or the mind, his ideas around which all his activities revolve.

All these "selves" are passing selves in time and space and ever changing in color and form. The self, or the ego, that is identified with these three worlds is mortal and must be "crucified" so that the real individuality, the real Self, may be resurrected. Herein lies the key to some mysterious words to be found in ancient writings. We read in the New Testament that "one must lose his self to find it...take off the old man with his deeds, and put on the new man"..."Take your cross and follow me." There are similar words in Buddhist Literature: "Take the

---

1. 2 Cor. 3:17-18.

Self as a lamp, take the Self as a refuge, material shape is impermanent. What is impermanent, that is suffering. What is suffering, that is not the Self. *What is not the SELF, that is not mine, that I am not, that is not my self.*" The words of the New Testament refer to the self which is matter, desire, thought or concept, or the sum-total of these. This self must "die" or be transfigured. It must die as the "old Adam" and be resurrected as the "new Adam."

The words of Buddhism refer to the Greater Self or the Higher Self in which all fires of the personal, lower selves are extinguished. The fires of the reflected selves must die out before man may rise to his source, his essence. The man is identified with the *reflection* of the true Self Who reflects Himself in the space of the lower states of substance, which we call personality, or lower self. Man must rid himself of this "ignorance," of this slavery, and become the Self which is light and freedom, and become all-inclusive. The process of extinguishing these small selves and of identifying with the Higher Self, is presented for us by Christ in three episodes.

1. As a youth, when he sat in the Temple in the midst of the doctors, He said to His mother, "Wist ye not that I must be about my *Father's business?*"

2. When He was on the Mountain of Transfiguration... The lower self became transfigured in the light of the Higher Self.

3. When He was on the Mount of Olives, in His deepest crisis, He said: *"Not my will, but Thine be done."*

The Masters of Wisdom say that the three disciples at the time of transfiguration symbolize the three worlds of human endeavor, the personality or the lower self. Christ symbolized the WAY or the Soul-infused personality, the transfigured personality at which time "the voice of the Father," the voice of the real Self, was heard. The reflection heard the VOICE of its Source—this was illumination, the annihilation of ignorance. How deep are the words of Christ—"The Father is in me, and I am in you." Here the man identifies himself with the Cause, and ceases to become an effect, a result; he ceases to become the plaything of the conditions and the affairs of the world. Again, it is worthwhile to remember the words of Paul:

"For now we see through a glass (mirror) darkly; but then face to face."

The Soul works in the three worlds of personality and tries to carry on its plan through them. The Soul gradually sublimates the personality so that it can express its light, love and wisdom through the three bodies. This transmutation continues until the personality becomes the channel of the Soul; and man, "the reflection," releases himself from ignorance (from Matter, Time, Space and Force) and identifies himself with his essence.

The Plan of the Soul, in our present-day language, is "the high-calling" of the man. When the Plan is beginning to work out, we say that the man has talent; when the Plan is expressing itself in its full beauty, we say that the man is a genius. When a man is able to fulfill his "high-calling" and is expressing his talent, his genius, he has come a considerable distance on his long path of sublimation. Note that the high-calling is related to the personality. In the case of talent, man to a certain degree is integrated with the Soul; in the case of genius, man is partially *en rapport with his "Father in Heaven,"* with the divine Spark within him, with his true Self. This is the process of sublimation, transmutation and transfiguration in which the reflection, under the guidance of the Soul, gradually meets its divine essence.

The process of soul-infusion in the literature of mystics is called spiritual marriage. The bride is the purified, ornamented virgin in white robe who awaits the bridegroom. She is pure, holy, and endowed with various graces. The Bridegroom is the vision, the crown of his head, who will give him a new meaning, a new life and who says to her in a sweet voice:

"Behold, thou art fair, my love;
Behold, thou art fair...
There is no spot in thee,
Thou has taken away my heart...
How fair is thy love, my sister, my spouse
Thy lips, O my spouse, drop as the honeycomb."

And the spouse, the transfigured personality replies:

"I sleep, but my heart waketh;
It is the voice of my beloved that knocketh, saying,
Open to me, my sister, my love, my dove, my undefiled."[2]

In ancient mysteries, the performance of the ceremony of opening the door was very beautiful, and the description of it can be found in the literature of many nations. It was the ceremony of initiation, the ceremony of touching the inner reality, which is represented by the Bridegroom.

In an Oriental church this ceremony has a deep significance and is performed in a very mysterious way. A priest stands in front of a huge curtain, singing and asking to be taken in. From the inner side another priest, representing the Soul, asks him some questions. The priest on the outside, after giving the correct answers, enters, while the choir sings joyous hymns. This was referred to in the New Testament where we are told that the veil of the temple was "rent in twain" from top to bottom.

According to the Bible there was a tabernacle closed by the first veil, which held a candlestick, a table and showbread. Then there was a second veil, behind which was another tabernacle, called the Holy of Holies, containing the golden pot that held manna and Aaron's rod that had budded... Thus there was an innermost tabernacle called the Holy of Holies, another in front of it called the Sanctuary, and an outer court. We must consider also that only the high priest, symbolically the Soul, could enter into the Holy of Holies.

In this wonderful symbolism we have described for us:

a. The outer court—the personality and a veil.
b. The Sanctuary—the Soul, the Son and a veil.
c. The Holy of Holies—the divine Spark or the real spiritual man—
   where we can have direct contact with the Great Presence.

Man, to realize his own essence, throughout the ages, must rend these "veils" separating the personality from the Soul, and the Soul from the spiritual fire.

Let us repeat the words of Solomon who says: "My sister, my love, my dove, my undefiled, open to me..." and, at the same time, let us imagine the MASTER who knocks at the door. In the Bible, this picture is given to us in three wonderful

---

2. *Song of Solomon,* IV and V.

events: The first has already been mentioned. The second is found in the New Testament where He, the Master of the Bridegroom, is returning from the wedding and knocking at the door. The third description is more mysterious and beautiful, and is found in *Revelation*, where it is written:

> "Behold I stand at the door, and knock.
> If any man hear my voice and open the door,
> I will come in to him and will sup with
> him, and he with me."

All these symbols refer to the process of Soul-infusion whereby the personality becomes the embodiment of the beauty, inspiration and energy of the Soul, which expresses itself as knowledge, love and sacrifice. It is interesting to note that the door, or the veil is made not of wood, but of cloth, and may be opened from within or without.

In the Ancient Wisdom, we are told that the above-mentioned triplicity (personality, Soul and Divine Spark, or Pure Spirit) is separated, one part from another, by very subtle veils, which both link and separate them from one another. For the personality (the outer court), the existence of the first veil is a safety valve. Without the protection of the veil, the energies and inspirations coming from the soul would burn and destroy the personality. The veils also transmute the incoming or outgoing energies and forces according to the capacity of the personality and transmits them to the vehicles.

The ceremony of knocking at the door means communion which the Soul wants to establish with the personality when it finds that the latter is "undefiled" and can open the door, or is ready to receive spiritual energies. When the man hears the "knock" he is first an aspirant, then a disciple at the portal of initiation. Every knock on the door is a vision, an inspiration, an invitation to the personality.

In esoteric literature, these veils are called "the dwellers of the threshold" which close the entry into higher planes. The personality in itself is a veil. In the Ancient Wisdom, esoteric instructions are given which are called "bridge-building processes." The bridges are those lines of communication which are established when the gaps between the veils are bridged, or the curtains are destroyed. One span connects the integrated personality to soul-consciousness, another connects the soul-infused personality to the spiritual essence, and the last span ascends to the Spark. The spans though having separate links, are parts of the same bridge.[3]

In esoteric literature the completed bridge is called the Rainbow-Bridge through which man achieves continuity of consciousness: he can be aware of his Soul's activity, he can raise his consciousness to the astral and mental plane, he can achieve monadic communication, and he can register these on his brain all at the same time. Also, at will, he can enter into sleep and, emerging from his body, can consciously communicate with his fellow disciples and Souls and remember these events in detail in his waking consciousness.

In the ancient *Upanishads*, we find the following significant words:

"Whoever knows the Thread (the bridge) and the inner Ruler, knows God, knows the worlds, knows the souls, knows all."

---

3. Read about the veils in *Christ—The Avatar of Sacrificial Love* by H. Saraydarian, chap. 19.

CHAPTER 8

THE MYSTERY OF SPACE

What is that which was, is and will be: whether there is a Universe or not; whether there be gods or none? asks the esoteric Senzar Catechism. And the answer made is—Space.[1]

—H. P. B.

In the beginning was Space, ever-present and self-existent, the Shoreless Ocean of pure Life-Electricity. Space was Life. This Space-Life willed to transcend itself, to surpass itself, to live, TO BE; thus It created a limit in Itself and, in the Dawn of Existence, a part of Space descended and condensed through seven steps; and substance, the root of matter, emerged. It is a divine, hidden law that to transcend or to surpass itself, a deity, a man, or an atom must limit itself and then release itself. Limitation creates relativity, and relativity urges us to move and progress.

Ages passed, innumerable ages, and between the condensed, materialized Space, and the Real Space-Life a certain relationship, a certain activity sprang up. This relationship brought about a third factor which was neither total space nor total substance, but a mixture of both. This *mixture*, throughout long ages, developed in itself an awareness of relationship. It looked up to Space, looked at itself—and a sense of otherness was awakened in it.

There was now Space-Life, also Root-substance, and the "Relation between" which was a conscious entity. This "Relation between" was an Existence, the highest pole of which was Spirit and the lowest pole Matter. The spirit-aspect was the first differentiation of space. This relationship was the Cosmic Bridge between substance and space—Absolute space, "the Unknown Causeless Cause." The Bridge was as a Rainbow Bridge. It was cosmic consciousness with seven stages or main grades the first color of which was called spirit, and the last color matter. Spirit was 99% space, and matter was 1% space and 99% substance. Thus we can say that Spirit, the highest plane of Existence, was the representative of Primordial Substance.

Space is in everything, everywhere. It can never be divided. In everything, the space aspect of nature is the controlling factor. All forms and existences disappear like bubbles; only Space remains. We feel the existence of Space when there is form. But form is only a concretion of space—when it disintegrates only Space remains.

Many more ages passed, and through the relationship of these seven Planes of Existence emerged subtle forms which composed the prototype of *all* future forms. "Occultism teaches us that no form can be given to anything, either by nature or by man, whose ideal type does not already exist on the subjective plane."[2] These

---

1. H. P. Blavatsky, *The Secret Doctrine*, vol. I, p. 9.
2. *Ibid.*, p. 282.

prototypes, or ideal types in their totality, are called the Great Plan, and the parts of this plan, philosophically, are called "ideas."

Plato intuitively grasped some of these facts and imparted them to his disciples. Later, Plutarch said: "An idea is a being incorporeal which has no subsistence by itself, but gives figure and form unto shapeless matter and becomes the cause of manifestation."

Let us not forget that every plane has its own ideas, the totality of which is the PLAN. The higher the plane is, the higher are the ideas, until at the highest point of Existence, the PLAN merges into the purpose of the Absolute Space-Life. "As above so below."

A soul is an idea as are Solar Angels, Spirits, Lives and Gods. Seen from below, they are purposes. All existence is essentially an IDEA.

Upon the lower planes, adaptation and the survival of the fittest are processes of expressing ideas, or the adaptation of forms to their prototypes or their mother-ideas.

In *The Secret Doctrine* we read:

> "The whole order of nature evinces a progressive march towards a *higher life*. There is design in the action of the seemingly blindest forces. The whole process of evolution with its endless adaptations is a proof of this. The immutable laws that weed out the weak and feeble species, to make room for the strong, and which insure the 'survival of the fittest,' though so cruel in their immediate action—all are working toward the grand end. The very *fact* that adaptations *do* occur, that the fittest do survive in the struggle for existence, shows that what is called 'unconscious Nature' is in reality an aggregate of forces manipulated by semi-intelligent beings (Elementals) guided by High Planetary Spirits (Dhyan-Chohans), whose collective aggregate forms the manifested *Verbum* of the unmanifested LOGOS, and constitutes at one and the same time the MIND of the Universe and its immutable LAW."[3]

These ideas are like music played by Space upon the seven strings of Substance, the highest note of which is Pure-Spirit and the lowest matter. These ideas came into being when Space-Life and Substance met and Substance was impressed by the purpose of Space.

The mother of all prototypes of ideas or ideal forms was called by the ancients the Son, the Soul of the Universe, the Way, and the Medium between Spirit and matter—between Space and Substance. This was the Cosmic Christ crucified upon the Cross of Space between Spirit and Matter. Existence in its totality forms a universal unity charged with the purpose of Spirit and endowed with the qualities of Substance through which it can express the purpose of Spirit, the purpose of Space.

Throughout religious literature we read that the foundation of the universe was an act of sacrifice. Thus a part of Life or Space sacrifices by extinguishing itself, then descends into matter to express itself and to transcend itself.

Long, long ages ago, there came a time when the Universal Soul as a huge and

---

3. *Ibid.*, pp. 277-278.

unmeasurable *Cloud "precipitated."* This was the greatest victory of Creation, when the spiritualized substance or materialized spirit divided into particles to carry on the Act of Creativity and growth. Throughout the ages these particles or "drops," passing through numberless forms accumulating experience, reached the stages of self-consciousness...and became "the Sons of God" who saw the mystery of God in the mirror of matter and to some degree identified themselves with that mystery, their real essence. When some of these "Sons of God" reached a certain high degree of development they were called "Souls," sons of mind, or Solar Angels. They put the mental spark in the evolving man, and then incarnated in him to lead him into the heights of Divine Understanding and Creativity because at that time the man-form was no more than an animal in consciousness.

Incorporated in the form of man is the Spirit aspect and the matter aspect. The Solar Angel is the bridge which leads the Spirit-aspect of man towards life-space and uses the matter-aspect to carry out the purpose of *Space.* Gradually, with the help of the Solar Angel, the Spirit aspect in man gains total control over the various grades of matter, and the man develops a new consciousness of his own and "remembers" his Father's House. When this is accomplished, He becomes a Soul.

As with the human form, every form has its own "soul." A cell, a grain, a tree, an animal, a planet, a solar system, a constellation—each has its own soul, its own bridge, which transmutes spirit into matter, matter into spirit, and furthers the Divine Plan. When this bridge, the soul, acquires self-consciousness and achieves a high degree of self-determination, it becomes a Solar Angel; "A superman, the lightning out of the dark cloud—man."[4]

From esoteric literature, we learn that there are nine initiations which the shadow in the personality must undergo before it becomes one with its source or prototype. A "Soul" in this process of initiation is one who has passed the fifth Initiation. He has become a Master of Wisdom and has gained victory over death. Thus, the One who lives in and around us as our Guardian Angel, our Soul, is One who passed through human experiences on this or another planet and, under the Law of Sacrifice, "descended" into man to carry on the process of spiritualization both in man and in Himself.

We are not yet Souls. We will become Souls when, through our Solar Angel, we will have established a certain relationship with our Inner God—with our essence—or with the highest principle in us and have brought our body and life under the rule of that Divine Reality.

In The Secret Doctrine we read the following beautiful words: "Matter is the vehicle for the manifestations of soul on this plane of existence, and soul is the vehicle on a higher plane for the manifestation of spirit, and these three are a trinity synthesized by Life which pervades them all."[5] Here another question comes to our minds. Are not our Divine Sparks and Souls the same thing? The answer is: The Soul on the plane of Its achievement separately carried on Its own development, Its own spiritualization. It aspires towards its own Spark, towards its Essence, towards Its spiritual principle while at the same time, It serves as a bridge between our Spirit and Its reflection—the man.

---

4. Friedrich Nietsche, *Thus Spake Zarathustra.*
5. H. P. Blavatsky, *The Secret Doctrine,* vol. I, p. 49.

We live as personalities or as reflections "as in a mirror" by the life and consciousness which we draw from our Souls. We aspire towards the Soul, towards soul-consciousness—the Soul aspires toward the Spirit. This process continues from incarnation to incarnation, until man comes in contact with his spiritual principle and gains victory over the matter aspect of his nature. Having achieved this, the Soul stands aside and proceeds to Its more advanced duties.

The Solar Angel feels a deep joy when the time for Its release approaches. This is also the time of release for man who now enters into the "kingdom of Souls." This is the law; no one can make real progress until he prepares someone to take his place. Such is the way to become divine.[6]

In the Egyptian *Book of the Dead* there is a wonderful hymn, referring to the above facts, in which the Deity says to man:

"I have given thee thy spirit

I have given thee thy soul

I have given thee thy *force.*" (personality)

"I have made my soul come and speak with his Father."

Through all ages, this trinity in man and in God forms the foundation of all religions and esoteric sciences.

To sum up this chapter, we can say that there is "an Omnipresent, Eternal, Boundless, and Immutable PRINCIPLE...beyond the range and reach of thought."[7] This is Space which is "uninfluenced by the presence or absence...of the objective universe." It is the one life, the unmanifested Deity. To quote the *Bhagavad-Gita* (10:42): "Having established this whole Universe with a fragment of myself; *I remain.*" The last word refers to Space or to the unmanifested Deity. The "fragment or portion" is Substance which emerged from Space. The relationship between *Substance* and *Space* brought out a third factor which we call the principle of Consciousness or the Universal Soul—the positive pole of which is *Spirit*, and the negative pole, matter.

This Universal or Cosmic Soul precipitated and became manifold. These drops of soul, or the mixture of substance and Space-Life, as they grew, gradually developed a consciousness of their own. And there came a time when some of the individualized drops succeeded in being more spirit and less matter. They started to influence their environment and became the Lords of their circles, the great Lives of the planes, and the Rulers of planets and constellations. Let us remember that planets or constellations are the bodies of Great Entities who, on Cosmic levels, "reached the appropriate equilibrium between Matter and Spirit." They have not yet become true Spirits. When they become absolutely pure, they enter into the Unmanifested aspect of the absolute Existence—Space. All Cosmic and universal laws have their origin in these Lords, Rulers and Existences because laws are "the imposition (upon the lesser and more important) of the will and purpose of that which is superlatively great"...*Our Solar Angels are the representatives in us of divine laws.*

6. Read *Cosmos in Man* by H. Saraydarian.
7. H. P. Blavatsky, *The Secret Doctrine*, vol. I. p. 14.

All atoms, cells and forms have inherited the qualities of the Universal Soul. Every atom, every cell is self-governed, has laws, has its own consciousness, sensitivity and discriminative power. We are told also that:

> "Every form on earth, and every speck (atom) in Space strives in its efforts towards self-formation, to follow the model placed for it in the 'HEAVENLY MAN'...Its (the atom's) involution and evolution, its external and internal growth and development, have all one and the same object—man."[8]

> "All in Nature tends to become Man."[9]

---

8. *Ibid.*, p. 183.
9. *Ibid.*, p. 170.

CHAPTER 9

THE SOUL AND ITS VEHICLES

The cosmic consciousness is reflected in all world structures. Only humanity is limited by inability to admit the integrity of existence. All points touch each other in Cosmos.[1]

—M.M.

As we have seen from the relationship of Space and substance, there emerged a bridge which we called the Soul of the Universe. The souls of men were the components of the Universal Soul. This middle point, the Great Soul which is now conscious, as it emerged deepened its relationship towards space and substance, or towards its spirit-pole and matter-pole, and thus created a ladder of relationship. It may be compared to a tree which spreads its roots towards substance and its branches towards space.[2]

This process of extension produced the Seven Cosmic Planes, which are referred to in ancient literature as Seven Planes Relationship. To clarify this, a unit upon the lowest density needs seven Cosmic stages to reach the highest subtlety or "Spirit," and the highest unit of subtlety needs seven steps to reach the lowest state of inertia or matter. Upon this ladder, the spirit-pole (which is more space than substance), descends into matter, and matter (which is more substance than space), ascends toward the state of Spirit. The Universal Soul is conscious of these seven Cosmic Planes, the lowest of which is the Cosmic physical plane.

The precipitated drops, units or souls which were half matter and half Spirit, through the ages gradually gained conscious mastery over the planes of the Universal Soul, developing in themselves the potential of latent planes. The central core of these drops was composed of a circle of a rare substance of spirit in which there was a "jewel" of *Space,* of unknown Deity. The subplanes of our cosmic physical plane are formed by the relationship of Spirit and matter, or substance and Space. They are graduated as follows:

The upper four planes, which are more Spirit than matter, are called the four cosmic etheric planes; the lower three, gaseous, the liquid and the dense physical planes. In esoteric literature they are called:

1. The first cosmic etheric plane.
2. The second cosmic etheric plane.
3. The third cosmic etheric plane.
4. The fourth cosmic etheric plane or the plane of the intuition
5. Mental plane
6. Emotional plane
7. Physical plane

---

1. The Agni Yoga Society, *Infinity,* p. 164.
2. See *The Science of Becoming Oneself* by H. Saraydarian, pp. 13-14, 130-156.

The physical plane is divided as follows:

1. 1st ether
2. 2nd ether
3. 3rd ether
4. 4th ether
5. Gaseous
6. Liquid
7. Dense physical

The higher planes are also divided into seven sub-planes according to their relative density or spirituality.

The Solar Angels that came to man and incarnated in him, located in the three highest sub-planes of the mental plane and became the Soul of man. To the Solar Angels the mind, the emotional vehicle and the physical body, with its senses, are windows of relationship through which They come in contact with the matter of these planes, enrich Their experience and are enabled to express Themselves.

The Soul is a bridge both in man and the universe. It is the Son who leads us towards the Father's House.

The physical and other subtle bodies of man are built by the substance of the seven planes of Cosmic physical plane.

The physical body that comes into existence during pregnancy is the densest vehicle of the human soul through which the human soul will come in touch with the material world. Before pregnancy, the soul is endowed with the blueprints of its mental, emotional and other potential bodies. At the time of conception it starts to build its physical body. Under psychological testing, some people have recalled experiences which occurred while they were in their mother's wombs.

Potential parents consummating sex are not creating a new soul, but are preparing the atmosphere, the substance, in which and through which the soul is building its form. From birth until age seven, the soul tries to subjugate the physical body; from seven to fourteen, it takes similar action upon the emotional or astral body; and from fourteen to twenty-one, it endeavors to use and control the mental body. At age twenty-one another cycle starts during which the soul deepens its influence over these three bodies.

At the time of death, the soul leaves the physical body to reside in the emotional body; later, it leaves the emotional body and resides in the mental body; and still later it reincarnates.[3] Kahlil Gibran, at the end of his book *The Prophet*, says, "A little while, a moment of rest upon the wind, and another woman shall bear me." Michael Naimy, in his wonderful book *Mirdad*, writes, "When you pass out of the cycle known as life into the cycle known as death and carry with you thirst unquenched for the earth and hungers unappeased for its passions, then will the magnet of the Earth draw you again to its bosom. And the Earth shall suckle you and time shall wean you, life after life and death after death, until you wean yourself once and for all of your own will and accord."

The Koran, Surah II:28 says, "How disbelieve ye in Allah when you were dead, and He gave life to you! Then He will give you death. Then life again, and then unto Him you will return."

---

3. Read *Cosmos in Man* by H. Saraydarian, chap. 19 "The Process of Death and Life After."

Paul refers to these bodies in his Epistles and calls them "natural body" and "spiritual body." The physical body is also known as "an earthly home," "earthen vessel," "tabernacle;" and the subtler bodies are called "house, eternal in the heavens," "celestial bodies," "bodies of glory." At the time of death the soul separates itself from the physical body, or as Peter says, "puts off this tabernacle" and carries the subtle bodies away with it. The soul now has an emotional body and a mental body to relate with the corresponding planes of the universe, as it functioned on the physical plane with its physical body.

When a man is advanced spiritually he can, as a soul, consciously leave his body and rise to higher planes of being. By the advanced process of contemplation and trance, he can gradually draw himself out of his lower bodies and come in contact with higher planes. Sa'adi, the Eastern poet, in the following lines refers to this, "One of the mystics, through deepest meditation, submerged himself into the ocean of God; when he returned, one of his friends asked him, 'What did you bring us down from Heaven where you went?' He said, 'I was intending to bring you roses from the bush, but when I reached there, I lost myself in the smell of the rose...and did not bring anything to you.'"

"Rapture," says Saint Teresa, "comes in general as a shock, quick and sharp, before you can collect your thoughts or help yourself in any way; and you see and feel it as a cloud or a strong eagle rising upwards and carrying you away on its wings...during Rapture, the body is very often as if it were dead, perfectly powerless...Sometimes the person is at once deprived of all the senses, the hands and the body becoming as cold as if the soul had fled; occasionally no breathing can be detected..."[4]

A very beautiful classic example is given in Buddhistic literature concerning the withdrawal of the soul. We are told that "the All-Enlightened One" addressed the brethren saying, "Decay is inherent in all component things, work out your own salvation with diligence." These were the last words of Buddha. Thereafter, He entered the first of the higher states of consciousness and then the second, the third and the fourth. He passed still further into the realms of awareness where none but a Buddha enters: "Thus, Gautama, the Buddha, ended His last incarnation and passed from the eyes of man."[5]

In esoteric literature the process of passing on to higher levels is called *Ascension,* in which there are four degrees.

1. In the first degree the man detaches himself from the physical plane, or body.

2. In the second degree, the unit of awareness is withdrawn from the emotional world.

3. In the third degree, the unit of awareness withdraws from the world of thought-forms, from the mental body.

4. In the fourth degree the man penetrates into the "fourth" plane which is called the Intuitional Plane.

Masterpieces of literature and music, lofty ideas, inventions, and visions are

---

4. E. Underhill, *Mysticism,* pp. 376-378.
5. Christmas Humphreys, *Buddhism,* pp. 41-43.

the fruits of people who are able to penetrate into the intuitional plane. The ascension, or rapture, is of two kinds. First the awareness unit gradually emerges into a divine joy and light and, upon returning to its natural state of awareness, remembers nothing, but feels very happy and content. Second, the man is more conscious. He has aligned his bodies and built the bridge through which he can record higher impressions with the brain. In the first case, the man is a mystic, in the second, he is an *occultist*. Only through meditation and dedicated service can we enter the higher states of consciousness and bring new light, new laws, new inspiration to lead our race and humanity "from unreality to reality." Dr. Alexis Carrel writes, "Great scientists always have profound intellectual honesty. They follow reality wherever led by it. The man who longs for the contemplation of truth, has to establish peace within himself. His mind should be like the still water of a lake."[6]

"It seems that everything reaching the brain has to enter the sensory organs, that is to influence the nervous layer enveloping our body. The unknown agent of telepathic communications is perhaps the only exception to this rule. In clairvoyance, it looks as though the subject directly grasps the external reality without the help of the usual nerve channels."[7] Thus, modern science slowly approaches the field of esoteric knowledge.

The Ancient Wisdom taught that man has not five senses but seven, and he is able to consciously withdraw himself from the lower planes and enter higher planes where he can use his higher senses to communicate *with higher worlds.*

---

6. Alexis Carrel, *Man, the Unknown*, p. 233.
7. *Ibid.*, pp. 71-72.

CHAPTER 10

THE HEALER

After acquiring a body when the indweller wants to leave it, He takes his senses and goes away as the wind carries away the fragrance from the flowers.
                                              —*Bhagavad Gita* (15:8)

In the depths of the soul are to be found certain foci of light, upon which is registered the sum-total of all experiences and stages of achievement gained during the periods of physical-plane life. As a result of the vibration of these foci, when a man incarnates he takes a physical body, an emotional body and a mental body. When these foci, or the seeds of the bodies, have higher vibrations they create purer bodies, stronger bodies, or more sensitive bodies. In other words, the man's body will be the result of the seeds he has sown in past incarnation. Because we reap what we sow, the results of our mental, emotional and physical deeds are gathered or impressed upon these inner centers, and they will bear fruit accordingly in our future bodies. For example, if one breaks the law in any way and does not pay the price in that life, he will have to pay it during a future incarnation. Every act, feeling and thought is registered in "the Book of God." In Buddhist literature, we find these significant words: "All that we are is the result of what we have thought, it is founded on our thoughts, it is made up of our thoughts. If a man speaks or acts with an evil thought, pain follows him, *as the wheel follows the foot of the ox that draws the carriage.*"

In the field of psychology doctors have been faced with complicated problems. In many instances the roots of these problems do not lie in our present life, but in one of our previous incarnations. In order to heal a man, doctors may one day try to eliminate the causes of affliction which were the results of his misdeeds during his previous lives. Through psychological therapy, or by medication, it is possible to cure some illnesses temporarily, but if the roots of the illnesses are not burned out, in time they will become stronger, grow, and one day return in the form of new and more complicated illnesses or diseases.

Through hypnotism at present, doctors are trying to heal many diseases and are slowly making strides in this field. From the viewpoint of esotericism, however, hypnotism is a very dangerous tool and the harm it does may be very deep and wide-spread. Dr. Ron Hubbard says, "Hypnotism as a parlour game, is a thing which no society should tolerate, for it may be sufficiently destructive to cause the engrams to restimulate to a point of insanity." (*Dianetics,* p. 350)

Hypnotism destroys the self-determination of the subject and prevents the release of soul-energy, creating walls between the planes of mind, emotion and the higher states of man. It suppresses "certain physical and mental disorders." For example, let us take the case of a young man whose left hand was paralyzed. He consulted a hypnotist who affected a cure. A few months later, he developed leg-paralysis and the same hypnotist healed him. A few weeks later he lost his voice and upon returning to the hypnotist, regained it. Shortly thereafter he was hospitalized entirely blind. One of the subtle bodies of the man had a "wound," an engram, or a complex, which was seeking to emerge and exhaust itself.

Hypnotism suppressed it, did not allow it to express itself. At best, hypnotism may cut the branches of an illness, but the roots remain in the subtle bodies of men.[1]

There is a wide field of investigation into the human composition. Man is not only a physical body, but has emotional and mental bodies and even subtler bodies as well. If one of them is hurt in any way, it develops a very complicated wound. This "wound" in due time expresses itself in the form of psychological or physical disease. True healing should not be limited solely to the physical plane, but must include all the vehicles of the soul.

When we speak of "psychological healing," many people believe we refer to the soul, but this is not so. It is not the soul which becomes ill, but its vehicles. Advanced studies in psychosomatic medicine indicate that 75% of human illnesses have their origin in the world of human emotions and thought; or in the mental and emotional planes or vehicles of the soul. When a disturbance occurs on these planes, the life current cannot circulate freely throughout the mechanism of the man. It accumulates at certain locations, creating overstimulation or understimulation, thus causing many complicated diseases.

In *Esoteric Healing*, the Tibetan Master says, "All disease is the result of inhibited soul life, and this is true of all forms in all kingdoms. The art of the healer consists in releasing the soul, so that its life can flow through the aggregate of organisms which constitute any particular form."

At present a group of psychologists and psychiatrists, with the help of esoteric students, are working on a system to produce soul release and radiation. Along this line psychosynthesis has made a fine beginning. Through testing and experiences, it has become apparent that psychosomatic illness is the result of an inner, distorted vibration which exists in the subtle bodies and gradually emerges in the form of a malfunction. However, if the causes of illness have not exhausted themselves through the physical body at the time of death, then on the death of the other bodies these existing causes register themselves in the seed-atoms found in the atmosphere of the soul. When the soul again tries to develop the threefold man, these traces or vibrations create disturbances which cause diseases in the subtle bodies. In due time these diseases express themselves on the physical plane.

Sometimes, a physical illness is advantageous, because through that illness some inner disturbance is releasing and exhausting itself. When a hypnotist tries to stop or suppress the illness the inner cause deepens and becomes more dangerous, because naturally the illness will express itself some day and this time it may cause more damage to the man and to the environment. In order to affect a complete cure, the aim of the highest form of healing will be directed to the inner causes. If they can be eliminated, then it may be possible to have perfect health for humanity. Incidentally, all religions have a therapeutic value because they encourage living a life which automatically releases the energies of the soul. They encourage man to live through his threefold bodies, in harmony with the Inner Light, so that he does not create bad karma or inhibit the soul life.

It is clear that the foci of light are the atoms from which our future bodies and characters are formed. They are the seeds of our future physical, emotional and mental achievements. They automatically create our bodies according to our *merit* "and distribute certain types of forces." We can change vibrations in future incarnations by living more nobly in this life, with lofty ideas and selfless service

---

1. Read *Cosmos in Man* by H. Saraydarian, chap. 14, pp. 135-138 on hypnotism.

to our race and humanity. Sudden cures have been cited where the cause of illness exhausts itself through intense faith and aspiration, or through a soul release which eliminates causes found either in subtler bodies or in the life-atoms. Dr. Alexis Carrel says that "Miraculous cures occur despite their small numbers; they prove the existence of organic and mental processes that we do not know. They show that certain mystic states, such as that of prayer, have definite effects." He also says, "Our present conception of influence of prayer upon physical lesions is based upon the observations of patients who have been cured almost instantaneously of various afflictions such as peritoneal tuberculosis, cold abscesses, osteitis, suppurating wounds, lupus, cancer—often an acute pain, then a sudden sensation of being cured. The only condition indispensable to the occurrence of the phenomenon is *prayer*, but there is no need for the patient himself to pray or even to have any religious faith. It is sufficient that someone around him be in a state of prayer. Such facts are of profound significance."[2]

It is not our intention to emphasize miraculous cures, but to show that outer bodies are in reality the true shadows of inner states of being. On changing the inner state, a corresponding change occurs in the physical body. The reader may ask a question here. Perhaps he has read that some holy men and women suffer deeply. Why is this, if our sufferings are the results of inner causes? Even a man who lives a dedicated life may have sown "tares" in his "garden" in past incarnations. His holiness in this life can create a convenient atmosphere through which his past engrams, inner wounds, more quickly exhaust themselves and create a very complicated situation for him. But he can be sure that the future will hold good for him. It is also true that the vibrations of a holy, spiritually-advanced man can affect the atmosphere around him and cleanse it from many disturbing influences, because everything in existence is vibration. A strong vibration can transmute a body that has a lower vibration; it can also destroy it. Highly moral and spiritual people are usually immune to contagious disease, because their strong magnetic and radioactive atmosphere protects them and their environment.

A soul is a sinless entity. It cannot be sick or ill. The causes of illness are not found in the human soul, but in the bodies. The reflection of the spark of life which exists in the lower bodies may sin and break the Good Law, the Law of Love. This reflection may pay the karma and gradually advance on the path. When this reflection has reached the stage of soul-infusion, has been tested in the fire, has emerged as pure gold, it has become a Master of Wisdom and a fountain of light, love and power. The evil man, the harmful one—he who complicates the lives of others, causing them suffering and trouble, and preventing the progress of his fellowman—is a man who is not yet a Soul or in contact with his Soul or with his Solar Angel.

Human soul is the subjective Sun living in the bodies; It is the pure rhythm, the power station from which all graces and all creative beauties may radiate. All beauty, health and creativity will belong to those who purify the atmosphere of the soul and release its glory.

"Unseen, she sees, unheard she hears, unminded, she minds, unknown, she knows. There is none that sees, but she, there is none that hears, but she, there is none that minds, but she, there is none that knows, but she. She is the soul, the inner ruler, immortal. Whatever is different from her is perishable."[3]

2. Alexis Carrel, *Man the Unknown*, pp. 141-143.
3. *Brihadâranyaka Upanishad*, verse 23.

CHAPTER 11

THE APPEARANCE OF THE SOUL

Withhold thy mind from all external objects, all external sights. Withhold internal images, lest on thy Soul-light a dark shadow they should cast.[1]
—H. P. B.

Since the dawn of humanity stories have been told about "the souls" who have appeared under diverse conditions and for many purposes. The subject is discussed widely in Holy Books and in religious and mystical literature. Shakespeare, in *Hamlet,* in a very clear and beautiful way condenses these traditions and stories when he has the "soul" of the poisoned king appear to Hamlet and reveal some secrets.

There are many stories of people who state they have seen saints, masters or great religious leaders in ethereal simple or very luminous form. Others report that they have seen angels and messengers of God in human form. Most of these angels have wings, long hair, and hold a symbolic object such as a rose, lily, a spear or an olive branch.

These stories have led people to believe that the soul has a human form and that after death man retains his human appearance. We have heard of someone who said, referring to a deceased loved one, "I saw him in my dreams. He spoke to me." Unconsciously the dreamer was thinking about the soul of his friend communicating with him. He imagined that his friend, on leaving his body had become a soul, but had retained the same appearance and form that he had in life, only of finer substance. It seems that out of this superstition came the idea that God has the appearance of man. Thus He created man according to His image and likeness—as God is portrayed for us by many artists.

In the ancient mysteries of Egypt, the soul was depicted as a bird hovering over the body, or as a butterfly emerging from a caterpillar. In spiritualistic circles, the "soul" often "appears" in human form, and people believe that they see human entities or souls or "spirits." There are also traditions in which people have seen the "souls" of the dead in graveyards in human form with luminous appearance.

We cannot say that all these visions belong in the world of illusion. People are prone to translate all unexplainable phenomena into a familiar language and color it according to their current state of mind. Generally in such cases their psychological world is composed of strong aspirations, dreams, fears and desires. All these condition the appearance or form of the "vision." People sometimes see things which are mere reflections of the "realities" within themselves. The atmosphere of their minds helps this process and gives form and color to their dreams and fears. This law of psychology also says that we perceive that quality and character in an object which already has been developed in us. Hence, people usually ascribe to the soul a human form.

---

1. H. P. Blavatsky, *The Voice of the Silence.*

46

These forms and appearances are divided into seven principal categories:

A. First we have the simple forms, somewhat like shadows which are created by the thoughts and desires of people. These forms may live for many years. According to esoteric science, our thoughts have forms and colors and are built of very subtle mental, emotional and etheric substances.

For example, when we think of an object, it gradually assumes a subtle form, which is beyond the visible range. In all creative activities, we first build the prototype which later materializes and takes form upon the physical plane. It sometimes happens that, due to improper conditions, the prototype cannot materialize and so remains as a nebulous form in space. This gradually organizes itself and becomes stronger in the dreams and thoughts of people who think along these lines. Sometimes, this is the case when we think we see the "soul." Through the power of love, anxiety, or concentrated thought, the subtle form of a beloved one in the subjective world may be envisioned under "unnatural" conditions, and we believe that it is the soul of the beloved one who has to come to see us or has an important message to impart. These forms may speak, sing, shout, or transport objects. This is not a mystery to the student of Ageless Wisdom, who knows that some discarnate entities can adopt such forms, use them as vehicles, and contact people who are in tune with them. Without these forms, the entities would not so easily be able to come in contact with the physical world.

Thought-forms can be built in several ways. Once they come into existence and float in space, they spread their good or bad influence in the area surrounding them affecting the minds and hearts of the people they contact. A person who has strong sexual *appetites* may continuously build or create "objects" of his or her desires. These "objects" or thought-forms gradually gain strength, color and shape, and become condensed. After a while, men or women living in the environment of this person may experience unnatural appetites and urges. The urges gradually become stronger and gain control of the activities of these people, leading them into shameful or illegal relationships. Should they try to control such urges, they may be led into prolonged fasting or intense inner conflicts may result. It is not a miracle which is happening but the created thought-forms, with their vibrations, awaken similar tendencies in the minds of the people and force them to think or feel in the same ways. They then yield to the thought-forms.

In olden days, purity of heart was stressed because lofty ideas and visions affect the surroundings and create in them new, higher inspiration. An intense wish embodies itself through the substance and activity of the mind. A thought is substantial; it has its own life-period and influence. Some people clairvoyantly see these forms and, because generally the forms are human, people say they have seen "a soul" or a "spirit."

B. To the second category belong those appearances which are built up by the electro-magnetic atmosphere of the human body and personality.

The etheric body of a man has the same form as his body and it may decompose after death. The "spirit-forms," often seen in graveyards may have such an origin. Mixing with the phosphorus of the bones, the spirit-forms may take on a luminous, living appearance, especially when the inner state of the observer is full of fear, anxiety and other excitements. The physical body is the true shadow of this etheric, electro-magnetic field.

According to the esoteric sciences, first the etheric body takes form and then the physical body builds itself in the womb of the mother according to the blueprint of the embryo.

C. In the third category are found some "astral" appearances. In esoteric literature, we read that a dying man first departs from his physical body, and then leaves behind another body, called the "astral body."

The astral body has the color of silver, of a shining star. The shape of that body is similar to the physical one and when people see such a form, they think that they are meeting a luminous angel or an entity, but it is really only a shell. Sometimes, the real man may be present within it and may try to communicate with us when we are asleep. Generally, in sleep, we wear our astral body and communicate with the astral world; it sometimes happens, however, that some "spirits," "evil entities" or "earthbound souls" occupy this shell and use it for their own purposes. For example, they will try to use the astral form of a leader in order to convey to his friends or followers some wrong teaching, or give some wrong instruction, trying to destroy the band of followers. This often happens during a *spiritualistic* seance, and participators believe that they are receiving a true message from their beloved one who is now a "soul."

D. To the fourth category belong mental forms, or thought-forms, which are built by advanced souls who bring to humanity some message, or instruction.

An expert in the mental laws who has control over his mind, in imagination can create a thought-form of himself and then visualize this form going to a certain man, giving him some message and returning. Advanced individuals who are familiar with the principle of materialization can do the same thing, in order to give messages or instructions to their disciples and create in them desired states of consciousness.

People may say that they have seen a holy man, a saint, or a prophet. It is true that they saw something. However, 99% of the time it is not the person they believed they saw but his projected picture or thought-form. It is not a *soul* — only a form mentally controlled by the real subject.

Created forms live on indefinitely unless their creator destroys them by his occult power. When the forms are built strongly and charged with potent vibrations, they become visible to sensitive persons. It may also happen that such forms, by their own high vibrations, create sensitivity in those towards whom they are directed and create in them a temporary clairvoyance. Such an apparition, after fulfilling its role, multiplies in the imagination of a group of people and daily becomes stronger through the force of their aspiration and magnetism. Many duplications of this apparition may live on in that locality.

A great danger exists when evil or deceptive entities project themselves during the night when we are asleep. They may pass on to the sleeper special messages in the form of dreams or visions, show him new worlds or reveal pseudo-secrets to him. The receiver of these new messages, visions, or dreams becomes "a new man" the next day. He leaves his home and family to become "a savior," "a prophet" or "a leader"; he starts a new teaching. This man sincerely believes that a saint or an angel is projecting for him a sacred duty, which must be performed at any cost. No one can change his mind, because he is so possessed by ideas implanted by the entity that he cannot give credence to anything else. Such people may be seen, especially, in "holy cities." They have become mentally unbalanced, are isolated from the community, and live in a visionary state. They are cursed by their ignorance; they have become the victims of illusions and glamors. This illusion, through the same natural laws, creates a whirlpool which attracts and focuses the energy of the man or of the group in which it functions. A short time later the man caught in this whirlpool commences to reveal himself as an inspired leader, a messenger of God, or a savior of the nation. If he finds the proper atmosphere, he becomes a great danger which grows and later disappears like a dust devil. Such a "prophet" appeared some years ago in India. He was a "Persian," a man who had fallen into the net of his illusion. Another such prophet appeared in France, claiming to be one of the disciples of Jesus and, for a short period, attracted a group of followers who later disbanded. We have many of such people in the world. In the political arena, a good example of this phenomenon was Hitler who reached tremendous heights and later was discredited. He brought the deepest suffering and destruction not only to his nation but to the whole world.

It may happen that the "form" or apparition retains a connection with the possessed one until the latter becomes a victim of hopelessness and dies. To be safe from such attacks, some people read holy books and carry on their persons amulets, fetishes, symbols of the cross or five-pointed stars.

E. The subtle bodies of some advanced souls are found here. After the disintegration of the physical body, they retain their etheric, astral, and mental bodies, and if they have advanced sufficiently, these bodies are very subtle and beautiful.

It may happen that a real Saint, a real Savior, leaves one of his subtle bodies to a disciple of his, endowing him with the light of his achievement. A beautiful example of this process is given in the Bible, when Elijah leaves his mantle to Elisha. Elisha, upon receiving it, acquires Elijah's "spirit" or power.

In ancient mysteries, the mantle or clothing represented the subtle bodies of initiates. To put on a new garment or "robe" meant to enter into the consciousness of a new vehicle. In the Bible the following significant words are found:

"I will greatly rejoice in the Lord
My soul shall be joyful in my God;
For he hath *clothed* me
with the garments of salvation,
He has covered me
with the robe of righteousness."[2]

In the Bhagavad-Gita, bodies are represented symbolically as garments or

---

2. Isa. 11:10.

clothing. For example: "These bodies of the embodied One, who is eternal, inde-
structible and boundless, are known as finite...

"He who regardeth this (the Self) as a slayer and he who thinketh he is slain,
both of them are ignorant. He slayeth not, nor is he slain. . . .

"As a man casting off *worn-out* garments taketh *new ones*, so the dweller in
the body, casting off worn-out bodies, *entereth into others that are new.*"

In the present century scientists are studying the possibility of transferring
knowledge from one man to another, as electricity is transferred from one body to
another. According to the Ancient Wisdom, this is not an unachievable dream
when we remember that our bodies are conveyers of light and wisdom.

> F. To this category, belong the real entities who appear during periods of
> great national and international crises and needs. These entities are
> not in the flesh but are to be found in their etheric bodies which
> resemble their physical bodies.

The soul, the entity or the dweller in this etheric body, enters into relationship
with people whose bodies are refined and pure, and who can endure strong vibrations. It may happen, however, that when the aspirant is not ready, such contact
results in a nervous or glandular breakdown; some mystics and spiritual people
experience strange moods and states of health.

Advanced entities, usually called MASTERS, can appear in their etheric, more
glorious bodies of radiant and colorful beauty.

> G. Here we have the true appearances which have real physical bodies,
> but in a more sublimated state.

The Masters of Wisdom often appear in their physical bodies to their disciples
and convey to them the teaching for coming ages. Here also, however, people may
become the victims of their selfishness and illusions. They see an apparition and
believe that a Master or a prophet is approaching them with some advice regarding
their petty, small selves.

It is an esoteric rule that Masters appear only at the time of a national, group or
universal need. They are not interested in devotional people but seek intelligent
persons capable of receiving instructions to be transferred to mankind.

In the objective world, as in the subjective world, there exists the real, and
with it the unreal; the true, and the false. The aspirant to the mysteries can pass
over this trial bridge by the light of *his intuition, but only if he has sufficiently
developed his mental powers.*

All of the categories discussed in this chapter refer to appearances which
people accept as the appearance of the "soul" or the form of the soul, whereas in
reality, they are outer appearances. What is the true appearance of the soul un-
veiled and without its vehicles?

CHAPTER 12

THE INNER LOTUS AND THE SOLAR ANGEL

Know the Soul. It is the bridge which leads to immortal Being.
—Upanishad

Energy can express itself in many ways. On the physical plane it may take the form of activity; upon the emotional plane it may express itself as desire or wishful thinking; on the mental plane it may appear as a thought; and upon the other higher planes, as a vision, an idea, or a purpose. If we ascent higher still, it can express itself as intuition and pure will.

It is the same energy, but it adopts diverse qualities and appearances as it comes in contact with different planes. Any given plane is responsible for the quality and the form of the expressed energy thereon. Hence, the expression of the energy reveals its source and the degree of achievement of the subject. This is also true of the power of perception. The unfoldment of consciousness is in reality a development of perception, or seeing; and the unfoldment of our vision is the measure of our achievement.

At present our vision can penetrate through many light-years; we can see very remote stars, even those that disintegrated many hundreds of years ago, and know their composition and history. We can also "see" the atom and the movements of its electrons.

This is also true of the esoteric field. Knowledge of self has its ageless history. As the individual ascends to the Real Self, his power to see and intelligence to grasp increase proportionally, and there comes a time when the functions of the senses become two-fold. The ears not only hear the outer voices but also the inner, or those voices and sounds which are beyond the scope of the audible range of vibrations of unenlightened individuals. The eye not only sees the outer object, but also the invisible, as waves of emotions and thoughts. A man who has sufficiently refined development can control his senses and use them for objective and subjective purposes. Gradually all the senses of man become synthesized in a higher sense, where hearing is equal to seeing, smelling, tasting, and touching.

For some people the Soul is the body, the flesh, and the blood. To others It is emotions and desires. For still others, It is thought, idea and mystery. Some people, who have departed from these familiar shores, have not arrived anywhere else, and the winds of events are conditioning their directions and state of life. Others have seen the way of light and, year by year, are growing in that light and entering into Soul-consciousness.

For simplifying abstract problems, the best tools are the language of analogy and the language of symbols. "Only a symbol can deliver a man from the slavery of words and formula and allow him to attain the possibility of thinking freely." Pure thought cannot be transmitted. It is necessary to clothe it with something.

The Soul is a unit of energy, a pure thought; but, when expressing Itself, It adopts a special appearance. Thus Its form and appearance, will be always relative or proportionate to the inner achievement. Close your eyes and envision a handful of fine powder, the molecules of which contain the seven principal colors of the spectrum. Throw that handful of powder into the air and let it take the form of a sphere in which innumerable molecules fly around at a very high rate of speed. A dark blue light streams forth from the center of that sphere. Stimulate your imagination a little more and visualize in what a wonderful way the molecules, magnetically held to the central core, are playing in the sphere, gradually creating rhythmic, harmonious waves and tones in which the yellow, silvery white, orange, light violet and red colors are clearly scintillating. The colors represent the planes of the Soul. These planes, according to their vibrations, take on different colors and, reacting to one another and to the impulses of the Soul, create beautiful forms or waves. After you have studied your created thought-forms for a moment, visualize the center itself where you will find *a point of blue light*, *a sun* which is composed of three rings: a ring of orange color, a ring of yellow, and one of blue. In the center you will find the *nucleus of absolute darkness* the center of *"light unapproachable."* Now, imagine that from that dark nucleus, "diamond," an energy is pouring forth, passing through the three rings and forming nine petals of a flower. The three petals are half open, the next three are unfolded a little more, and the outer ones are completely unfolded. Visualize this flower floating upon the *waters*. Let the flower project a stalk into the water and anchor itself into the mud with its roots. The space above the water represents the mental plane, the water is the emotional plane, and the mud is the physical plane.

The nine petals of the flower represent the nine fundamental radiations or energies which pour forth from the central diamond. They take the shape of tongues, and become the petals of the flower, of many colors and hues. These petals, each of which has its own rate of vibration and color, are etheric and luminous bodies which continuously radiate the influence of the rays coming from the nucleus.

In the Ageless Wisdom the third group of petals is called "knowledge petals," the second group is called "love-wisdom," and the first group is called "sacrifice." This wonderful flower, as a whole which we build in the higher mind is known as "The Temple Eternal in the Heavens." The higher mind in the Ageless Wisdom is called "heaven." Here is found the "Kingdom of God"—the Soul. This "building of God, a house not made with hands, eternal in the heavens," we have seven centers which resemble wheels and are found in our electromagnetic or etheric atmosphere outside the physical body along the spinal column—*above the seven main ductless glands*.

The Soul controls the bodies through the wheels, which in fact are its stations or centers of energy and consciousness. They, in turn, affect the glands and nervous system. Each center has the form of a lotus or lily, each endowed with its own colors, radiations, and rate of vibration.

For many centuries, a sacred Brotherhood has used the cross as a symbol. At the meeting point of the two arms of the cross, they have placed a rose as the symbol of the Soul. The vertical arm of the cross represents spiritual energy and the horizontal represents substance. Where these two arms cross, a whirlpool is produced which resembles a rose. This rose is the Soul, which bridges substance and spirit.

The lotus or lily has three inner petals which for a long time remain closed upon the central diamond; but when, after long ages, they start to unfold and radiate, their fiery essence burns the lotus formed by the remaining nine petals and annihilates it. Those inner three petals express the essence of spiritual life. The outer nine petals are divided into three tiers. To each personality-vehicle one of the petals from each of the three tiers extends, and here they spread knowledge, love and the will to sacrifice. Thus on the physical plane we have the influence of the first petals of knowledge, love and sacrifice; on the emotional plane, we have the second tier of petals; and, on the mental plane, we have the third petal of the knowledge petals, the third petal of the love petals, and the third petal of the sacrificial petals; this also holds true for the other planes of personality.

Upon each plane, the petals gradually and successively become active and effective until, upon the mental plane, the third petals of the third tier open. On this level, man becomes a living sacrifice and a source of light, love and power in his environment. The flower of the Soul has been unfolded and, if looked upon clairvoyantly, it will be seen that it has the supreme beauty of vibrating colors and radiation. This flower is situated just above the head of people who are spiritually advanced, and there it forms a crown of wonderful vibrations and colors which radiate love, wisdom, light and power in all directions. This flower turns upon its axis at a very high speed, and when the speed reaches its limit the unit of the central life is released and man has reached his goal. He has acquired a fourth-dimensional consciousness and is free from the limitations of space and time.

In the Ageless Wisdom, as afore-mentioned, the soul-flower is called the Temple of Solomon. This temple is built by "stones." The *Masons* actually prepare the stones with their "tools" and raise the temple towards God. These stones are man's good deeds, thoughts, and acts of love and sacrifice upon the three planes of personality. Each day of our life represents a stone which we are sanctifying to utilize in the building of this eternal temple in the heavens, in man and in humanity, wherein our God will live.

Upon the cross, Jesus symbolically represented this experience. He not only suffered in his body, but the "Temple" which was built by Him was in process of destruction. The curtain of the Temple was rent. The petals of the fourth tier, the central petals, which had started to unfold, were burning the Soul-flower, the Chalice. Then He cried, "My God, My God, for this I was spared." That was the CUP which He saw in the Garden of Gethsemane, when His "sweat was as if it was great drops of blood falling down to the ground." And, facing the whole mystery of Spirit, He said, "Not my will but Thy will be done." After the crucifixion, Jesus returned to His Father, becoming one with the will of God, because He had been able to destroy all the limitations of separative walls with His love nature.

Manu, one of the first lawgivers to Humanity, says, "The supreme duty of the man is to know his Soul, because that knowledge gives him the key to immortality. That man who recognizes the Great Soul within his soul, and within every creature...and who is rightful towards every man, towards every creature...he becomes a blissful man, and eventually merges into *the Heart of God*."

The lotus is the vehicle of the Solar Angel. It is in this lotus that the real individuality, the real Self of man is anchored, apart from the Solar Angel, as a flame which is partially extended and identified with the bodies. Each degree of identification creates a false "self," a false "I," known as the shadow or the reflection of the true Self, which is called the developing, unfolding human soul who, through liberation, goes back to "his Father" and becomes his true Self.

Every time man takes another step towards his central core, he awakens to his own reality, and a time comes when the radiation of his light synchronizes with the light of the Solar Angel. This event esoterically is called the divine marriage or Soul-infusion.

CHAPTER 13

APPROACHING THE SOUL

Selflessness attains, selfishness defeats; men's possibilities are in direct proportion to their ability to see beyond themselves and to feel for others.
—M. M.

How can we approach the Soul, the reality in us, and live our daily life in Its light, in the love and power of our Soul? At times we feel that we are a fountain of love, a source of light and power. We believe that we are pure as snow and that nothing can affect us, nothing can destroy us. We are full of joy and bliss. Then gradually the sun descends behind the mountains and we are again in the thickening darkness of our lower self, of our worldly life and its problems. Days and nights pass. We enjoy the blessings of light and experience the bitterness of the nights until our will becomes strong enough to stand in the light and to become one with it forever.

The first step in approaching the Soul is a life of service. The second step is the practice of meditation or the seven steps to illumination. The third step is a continuous living in the Soul light. Through these three steps, we approach our Soul and then our "Father in Heaven," to become one with Him. This is the true path along which, in all ages, people have passed to the joy of spirit, to the joy of service and of sacrifice. Our Soul is the only door through which we can enter into the spiritual world, come in contact with divine powers, and serve the Will of God. It is the first Initiator, the light in us and the representative of the Divine Plan.

It is impossible to attain our divinity, to reach perfection, without passing through the Soul and becoming a Soul. When we come in contact with our Soul, fuse with Its Light and grow as a Soul, then the mysteries will be revealed to our opening eyes, and the past, present and future will be ours. We shall become free Souls, free from time and matter, and will enjoy the presence of the ever-existent Light.

To walk towards the Light we must first of all cleanse our clothes, our personality vehicles, our physical bodies, emotional and thinking processes. Cleaning and purifying them means having a sound body; having emotions filled with love and sympathy towards every man; and possessing a clear-thinking mind, free from the fog of glamors and illusions, dedicated to study, meditation and creative activity. When our personality life is ready, we can commence the seven steps of illumination.

We are told that knowledge and relationships are possible only through the Light. If no light exists, there is no knowledge, no relationship, no experience and no growth. We recognize each other by light; we understand each other by the Light within. Look at the stars which palpitate in the immensity of the sky. We see them by their light, know their composition from the light, and also know their distances through the light.

Light is life, light is our guide. There are three Suns—the physical Sun, the subjective Sun, and the central Sun whence all things proceed. Every form has its own light and matter is a dim light. Each atom is materialized light; release the atom and you will see a blaze of light which will be transmuted into energy and disappear. The real man is a drop of light or of life. When that drop departs, the outer form, which is an extinguished light, will disintegrate. Should our sun die, no living form could remain upon the earth. We came from the Light and are returning to the Light. The path we are treading is the way of light which becomes gradually more illuminated. He who treads the Way is a drop of light. The source of that drop is the Light, as is the goal of that drop. All is Light.

In the Koran, there is a wonderful verse about the mysteries of Light and Soul, which says,

> "ALLAH is the light of the Heavens and the Earth. The similitude of His light is as a niche wherein is a lamp. The lamp is in a glass. The glass is as it were a shining star. This lamp is kindled from a blessed tree, an olive neither of the East nor of the West, whose oil would almost glow forth (of Itself) though no fire touched it. Light upon light, Allah guides unto His light whom He will. And Allah speaks to mankind in allegories, for Allah is the knower of all things." (Koran, Surah XXIV).

Matter is energy, and energy is light. The sun which we see is the light of matter; it is the clothing or body of the Real Sun, the Real Light.

People who see only their physical existence see only the physical world. The bodies in which they exist and the light of matter blind their vision to the existence of innumerable stars and suns. When the material sun has set, one can see the existence of the stars and other suns. A materialist is only aware of his existence; his vision is very limited. *Hence, every materialistic man tries to limit the freedom of his friends and fellowmen.*

Light is freedom. True freedom is the unlimited radiation of light. Every act against freedom is an act against the light, against the Soul. Man advances because light radiates. The inner light cannot stop radiating. It will grow increasingly destroying the walls of darkness and limitation. The inner light overcomes all limits. Gradually man realizes who he is and finds himself in the *Greater Light*.

The process of coming to know oneself is a process of becoming Light. The process of becoming Light is the process of overcoming the limits of matter, the limits of personality. Mind is the wind which fans the extinguishing "coal" into fire, into light. This is done through Meditation.

CHAPTER 14

MEDITATION

Meditation is a noble tool. It helps us to think, act, speak and write more creatively and in accordance with the highest good for all humanity.[1]

We are all on the path to self-discovery. On this path each of us is trying to find himself, to meet himself and to become a radiating Self. To advance on the path of conscious evolution the most important tool needed is meditation.

Meditation is a journey toward Oneself, toward the Inner Light, toward the Source of love and power within. *Without meditation* it is impossible to progress upon the path, because the path itself is a process of sublimation, of transformation. For example, you may buy beautiful, new furniture for your home, expecting that it will change your mood, your social relationships, your attitude toward life. It may help at first, but later you will find that you still have the same physical, emotional and mental problems as before. We often collect and store in our minds much "furniture" through reading, listening to the opinions of others, and gathering knowledge from many sources, but such accumulations are only "extra furniture," for it is through meditation that we find solutions to our problems.

Meditation is assimilation. We may eat good food, but if we do not assimilate it, it cannot provide nourishment to help us grow. Reading, listening and learning are all helpful; they may serve as "food," but if we do not meditate we cannot digest and assimilate them.

If we should decorate a large piece of charcoal with precious jewels and shining gold, it would still remain a lump of charcoal; it would not change. Without change there can be no progress on the path. The path is progress toward good; the path is sublimation; the path is transformation. If we strike a match and light the charcoal, it will begin to burn. When completely aflame it becomes transformed; it has passed through a process of transmutation.

Meditation may be compared to this process of change, of transmutation. Meditation increases your light, your love and your power, which are energies. Slowly, slowly, you come to realize that your body, your emotional world and your mental nature are changing.

There are hundreds of varieties of wood. Some are soft and pliable, others are brittle, yet others are hard and strong. Their use depends upon their quality. There is a wood so hard that it can be used to make needles for record players. The physical bodies of various people are also different. According to esoteric science our physical body can exist on any one of seven different levels. Our flesh manifests itself on its level. If our body is coarse and of low quality, we say that it is composed of sixth, fifth or fourth degree material. If sublimation is taking place within our physical body, the material of the body is changing. All the atoms, the tiny lives, the cells, change into a higher substance.

---

1. H. Saraydarian, *The Fiery Carriage and Drugs,* p. 75.

This is also true of our emotional body, our emotional world. Some believe that we *are* our emotions, that we *are* our feelings and that our emotional bodies are like waves of energy. Although it is true that they are waves of energy, they have a perfect structure similar to the physical body. Our emotional body, is composed of billions and billions of little lives. When we speak of our emotions, we are speaking of a mechanism that is like our physical body but of a more subtle nature. Through meditation all those tiny lives of lower order become sublimated, transformed and transmuted, allowing the Inner Light to shine through them more and more as they become clearer and purer.

The same principle may be applied to the mental world. The mind is not a shadow; it is composed of seven grades of substance. If your consciousness is working on the lower level of the mental plane your horizon is very limited, but if your consciousness is steadily focussing on higher and higher levels, sublimating all energies in the process, your horizon is expanding because you are coming closer to the real nucleus of life.

Meditation builds bridges within us. Sooner or later we discover that there are gaps between our physical, emotional and mental worlds. Meditation builds etheric bridges enabling you to become an instrument more sensitive to your environment; you become receptive to the impressions of the physical, emotional and mental worlds and register them in your nervous system. Until this sensitivity is achieved you are only half a person for you are not integrated or aligned; you are not yet a Personality.

Meditation performs another important function: it integrates and aligns the three lower bodies when they are integrated and aligned to a high degree, they become the Personality. Meditation puts the Personality in communication with the Soul, and that Inner Light begins to flow into the physical, emotional and mental bodies, molding them into a pattern which exists in the eye of the Thinker.

In meditation there are practical rules to follow. The following points will be of help to you in your meditation.

1. **Relaxation**
   Before starting your meditation it is essential that your body, emotions and mind become relaxed. Lie on your back and press your whole body firmly to the floor, tensing every muscle, do this for two or three minutes then relax the body. Now check all parts of the body, starting with the feet and moving upward from the toes until you reach the crown of the head. Wherever you find tenseness, concentrate on relaxing that part of the body. When you are completely relaxed imagine a black velvet curtain before your eyes. At the conclusion of this exercise, which takes about five minutes, you will discover that your physical body and your etheric or electromagnetic body are in closer communication with each other. Your etheric body is drawing more energy or prana from space and you are refreshed by the increased energy to the bodies and glands.

2. **Awakeness**
   To meditate one must be wide-awake; his brain and mind must be. alert. Sometimes people start to meditate when they are tired; their

minds are drowsy or unfocussed. They may fall asleep, or their minds may wander idly from one thought to another. To become alert we may use a simple technique. Kneel down, take a deep breath and, as you exhale, bow down and touch your forehead to the floor; holding the breath, remain in this position for ten or fifteen seconds and, as you inhale, slowly move back into the kneeling position sitting on your heels and exhale. Repeat this exercise three to five times. You will find that it refreshes and charges the brain with new energy, you now feel wide awake.

3. **Alignment**

The third step in meditation is alignment. Suppose you have three musical instruments: a violin, a guitar and a mandolin. Unless these instruments are in tune with each other they cannot produce harmony. Let us assume that my physical body is the violin; if the strings of my violin are not tuned I cannot play music. To play a selection, my violin must be in tune. To bring my physical body into harmony with the other two instruments, or bodies, it must be aligned. Am I sitting in a comfortable position? Am I relaxed? Is my spine erect? The principles of alignment which belong to the physical body also apply to the emotional and mental bodies.

When we have tuned the three "instruments" the physical body is completely relaxed, the emotional body is calm and peaceful, and the mind is detached from daily worries, work and occupations. When peace prevails in all three bodies, we must test to see that they are in tune with the fourth instrument, the piano.

Let us assume that the piano is the Inner Thinker, the Inner Light. To tune his three instruments with the piano, his three bodies with the Inner Light, the beginner will start by being calm, peaceful and detached. He will then imagine a great light shining down upon him; he will feel an intense desire to fuse with that light; he will visualize the light penetrating into his mind, his emotional nature and his physical body; and he will imagine that all three bodies are completely awake and in tune.

4. **Orientation**

The next step is to orient all these energies, to a great vision. Let us remember that our physical, emotional and mental bodies are units of energy and all these must be oriented to a high vision. It is possible to bring into focus our high vision through sounding the Great Invocation, the Gayatri or the "Lead Us Oh Lord":

THE GREAT INVOCATION

From the point of Light within the Mind of God
Let light stream forth into the minds of men.
Let Light descend on Earth.

From the point of Love within the Heart of God

Let love stream forth into the hearts of men.
May Christ return to Earth.

From the centre where the Will of God is known
Let purpose guide the little wills of men
The purpose which the Masters know and serve.

From the centre which we call the race of men
Let the Plan of Love and Light work out
And may it seal the door where evil dwells.
Let Light and Love and Power restore the Plan on Earth.

THE GAYATRI

OM
All you who are on earth, mid-Heaven and Heaven
Let us meditate
upon the light adorable
of the divine Sun of Life
which may enlighten our Souls.

LEAD US O LORD

Lead us O Lord
From darkness to Light,
From the unreal to the Real
From death to Immortality,
From chaos to Beauty.

By repeating one of these invocations in deep concentration about the meaning, you are lifting yourself up to higher dimensions as an airplane leaves the runway and propels itself upward into the sky.

5. **Sounding the OM**
The next step in your meditation is the sounding of the OM which is a very important mantram with far-reaching effects. When you sound the first OM its vibrations touch an inner center called the mental permanent atom. This center, which controls the mental body, becomes charged by the vibrations of the first OM. The vibrations of the second OM touch the emotional permanent atom, charging it. The third OM charges the physical permanent atom. Through these OMs a purification process takes place within these vehicles, and they synchronize themselves with the Inner Light.

The mental body becomes calm and oriented to the Inner Light; it becomes more sensitive to higher impressions.

The sounding of the OM also increases the sensitivity of the emotional body, washing away its fog, mist and "smog" which are technically called glamors; purifying the emotional body and making it ready to serve as a mirror for reflecting intuitional ideas. It is written that "There shall be no more sea." The sea represents the emotional body of man, of humanity and of the planet. The sea has become a mirror reflecting intuitional beauty which comes during meditation and permeates the emotional and mental bodies.

Without preparation for meditation, the ideas are lost for they cannot be registered nor impressed upon the bodies. The science of meditation brings us in tune, enabling these great impressions to come, to be registered and translated as clearly as possible. If the physical, emotional and mental bodies are not clean and prepared, the impressions come; but instead of bringing light they increase confusion; instead of uplifting, they stimulate lower energies and lead us into destructive activities.

It is man's mechanism that determines the expression of energy. For example, electricity is an energy. When this power expresses itself through a light bulb it illuminates; when it expresses itself through a refrigerator it produces cold; when it expresses itself through an iron, it emits heat. In each case the electrical energy, is the same, but the expression of that energy varies according to the vehicle of expression. If you are not ready, if you do not prepare yourself for meditation, the results are reversed. Instead of expanding your consciousness you focus it on your glamor, your illusions, your urges and drives, and you are led into confusion, but if you make the needed preparation, your path is clear and open, and slowly, slowly you will come to bloom—as do the lotuses and the lilies—in great beauty.

6. Meditation

After sounding the OM it is time to begin your meditation. Choose a single object or word, for example a pine tree. Examine it from the four viewpoints which the great sage Patanjali taught ten thousand years ago when he was dealing with the science of meditation. Patanjali taught that "The consciousness of an object is attained by concentration on its fourfold nature; the form, through examination, the quality through discrimination, the purpose through inspiration, and the cause or the soul through identification."

The history of the development of the human consciousness and the deepening of its understanding is the history of the four viewpoints from which we look at an object. A small boy has one dimension or viewpoint, he is interested in the outer form. As he grows he progresses to another viewpoint, he tries to find the quality of the object to use it for his ends; when he becomes a man he tries to find the purpose of the object; and when he reaches mental maturity he tries to find the cause of the object.

The Form. Let us take as an illustration the pine tree. Visualize its form and try to hear it. Lie down under it and listen to its music. Visualize its particular shade of green; notice its shape. As you do this you will discover many interesting things about the pine tree; you will begin to *know* it. A father once said to a great Italian artist, "I want my son to become an artist."

The artist replied, "Very well. Bring him to me."

On the boy's arrival, the wise man gave him a small glass bowl with a fish in it.

He said, "Look at the fish until I return."

An hour later he returned and asked, "How many fins does the fish have?"

"One," the lad replied.

"Ah!" said the artist, "I shall leave again, but this time pay more attention to the fish."

The boy began to examine the fish more closely but after a short time he thought, "I do not want to look at this fish anymore."

When the artist returned he asked. "Does the fish have eyelids?" The boy admitted that he had not observed.

"Ah," said the man, "How are you going to become an artist if you do not have concentration, observation, a seeing eye?"

This principle applies to the man who wishes to meditate. Preparing himself for meditation, he must examine his subject carefully and be able to answer any question concerning the object upon which he has been meditating. We are using the pine tree by way of illustration but we must understand that there are forms which are beyond our five senses. Our thoughts have forms; they are sometimes very beautiful, sometimes very ugly. Our emotions also have their special forms. Everything that vibrates, radiates or projects has a form; nothing exists in the universe without a form. Some forms last only a few minutes, some last for centuries. Forms which are in accord with the laws of Cosmos last a long time. To these forms belong high, lofty ideas, and positive emotions and feelings which are permeated with love and compassion. To know an object we must consider the form of that object. This is the first step of the scientific approach. Meditation is the maintaining of focused attention upon the object under consideration.

The Quality. The second step deals with quality. The quality of an object is that which differentiates it from another object. An apple is different from an orange. The gamma radiation is different from the beta radiation. Each man's character differs from the character of his neighbor.

Esoterically the word "quality" does not carry its contemporary meaning. In the Ancient Wisdom we are taught that everyone and everything—even ideas——have one of three qualities. In Sanskrit these qualities are called tamas, rajas and sattva. Tamas refers to inertia; rajas means the quality of motion; sattva is the quality of rhythm. Tamas, or inertia means inaction, very low, earthbound, dark. Rajas means motion alternating between light and darkness. Sattva is rhythmic motion, radioactivity. Through discrimination we find an object's quality which differentiates that object from other objects.

The Purpose. The purpose of an object is its destiny, the plan which it is preordained to fulfill. Every object, be it an atom, a man, a tree, a plant or whatever, has a purpose. The purpose of a form can be compared to a mosaic piece in the vast picture which the Great Architect is creating. The purpose of a form may be likened to a sound in the orchestra which is a part of the symphony of Cosmos. We may say that a certain man has talent, or is a genius. The talented person is he in whom the inner purpose is partially expressing itself; the genius is the man who is fulfilling that purpose completely.

The purpose is the inner direction of the object; it is the fulfillment of the object. When we examine the purpose of form we discover the plan of the architect and the dynamic principle which is called the *Cause of the form*.

Before we start to meditate we may think we know the purpose of an object; but as we meditate we find that we did not really know its purpose, or we may discover much, much more about it.

The Cause. Investigation leads to the cause of a form, whether it is a man or the universe, or even an emotion, an attitude, a mental state. If you find that you have come up against a wall which you cannot penetrate, do not be discouraged; persist, for this is your opportunity. Master Morya tells us, "Bless the obstacles; through them we grow."

To know an object, a man must have a synthesizing mind which simultaneously carries on its study of "objects" scientifically, psychologically, philosophically and spiritually. A man who meditates in this manner, eventually reaches the higher states of consciousness and steps onto the Path of Initiation leading him toward the mystery of a Greater Life.

The four view points, not only integrate the whole mental sphere, but also build bridges between the active consciousness and the storehouse of memories hidden in a corner of your inner departments.

How does this happen?

The objects that you are deeply meditating upon through four view points, will draw out from the inner storehouse those memories or impressions which are somewhat associated with the subject of your meditation. Thus many many forgotten events slowly will reappear on the surface of your consciousness, releasing tensions, or enriching your mind with past experiences. As you continue your meditation through four viewpoints, you will see that your ability to lecture, to solve problems, to bring needed experiences from the past into your conversation will increase greatly. Many people prepare their talks in writing, but cannot speak it, they forget. One who did long-time meditation, will not need to memorize his talks, because all that he thought and all that happened to him is available at any moment when he uses the right key of association.

You see some speakers, how they remember one after another many events, many stories or parables, connected with their main line of speech, as if they had a big bag in their head, ready with everything they need.

Meditation can also be an adjusting, cleansing and highly therapeutic process, as many suppressed or locked impressions release themselves and in the light and fire of meditation they burn away or dissolve, and greater urges and drives of service find way to be active and gradually express themselves in the life of the meditator, thus releasing him from a great tension and giving a deep sense of fulfillment and self-merit.

Besides these four view-points, which are very useful steps in raising our consciousness from level to level on the mental plane, we have another technique, which can be used especially by first ray people, or people who are interested in politics and rulership.

The following form of meditation, with its eight steps, tremendously expands our consciousness, if it is carried on systematically, day after day, and year after year.

Steps:

1. We take, as a seed thought any national, or world event, such as a war, a revolution, a political, economic or natural catastrophe, or great

events of peace agreements, great works of good will. Right human relations, international events of scientific, cultural, economic or religious cooperations or conferences, great acts of philanthrophy and so on.

2. Meditate upon your chosen seed thought, and try to find the cause of such an event. How did it originate, what factors helped to bring it into existence. Where are its roots extended?

3. After giving a considerable time to the step 2, go to the step 3 and think to find out the *effects* of such an event, upon you as a person, upon your family, group, or nation and upon all humanity. Try to find material, emotional, mental and spiritual effects.

4. In the next step you meditate about how such an event could be prevented, or can be repeated.

5. In the next step you will meditate to find out what relation that event has with the Hierarchical plan, or for the highest good of humanity. Is it an attack by some dark or materialistic, destructive forces upon any leader, group, nation or humanity, or is it a step forward towards progress.

6. How the *effect* of such an event can be obliterated, counteracted or perpetuated?

7. Do I have any prevision that a similar event may again take place in the future. What makes me think so?

8. What are the next immediate steps to be taken to create events that will help the growth and expansion of the consciousness of humanity?

Thinking or meditating upon these eight steps will stimulate our interest in the affairs of the world and create a greater sense of responsibility in our hearts, which will urge us to do our utmost to change those conditions of our life which work against freedom, health, prosperity, peace and joy.

The destructive or criminal events repeat themselves year after year because man does not think about their cause, and about the means to annihilate them. Such a meditation leads us towards knowledge and especially into action with its eight steps.

This meditation can be used very effectively in group discussion, or meditation.

During meditation we gradually raise our vibration. This gives us greater vision and greater communication, enabling us to progressively annihilate the barriers in our minds and enter into higher dimensions.

Meditation leads us to self-mastery and all mechanical and automatic functions of the mind come to an end, for example, dreaming. Dreaming slowly disappears as man goes deeper into the science and practice of meditation.

Most of our dreams are the symbolic interpretation of our wishes, desires, aspirations, fears, expectations, visions or they are the symbolic interpretation of some event which is taking place in the subjective nature or on a higher plane. When our consciousness expands and involves the higher plane through meditation, we put aside the source of our dreams that are originating from that plane. When we are consciously aware of our urges, drives, fears and aspirations, etc., we are able to meet them on a conscious level. They do not need to appear on our mental or astral planes through symbolic forms in dreams.

There are also dreams which are the result of some warnings or some imparted teachings. When we are aware of danger, we do not need warnings. When we reach the source of teaching and receive it directly from the source, itself, our dreams change into actual experiences.

When we are asleep on the emotional and mental planes, the impressions that reach us come from different sources which cause our dreams. As soon as we are awake on these levels, there is no need for an interpretation, hence no need for dreams. As a result of meditation we minimize our dreams. Meditation causes a continuous bridging process in our whole nature.

First the vehicles are aligned and integrated within themselves. Then the individual vehicles link themselves with the higher ones until Soul-infusion is achieved. Then the soul-infused Personality integrates itself with the spiritual realm, and then with the Spark in man.

A similar bridging process takes place, due to meditation between the individual and the group, between the individual and his master, the Hierarchy, the "Center where the Will of God is known," and gradually this bridging process extends towards the solar system and cosmos.

As man passes from one level to a higher one, the need of symbolic interpretation decreases, and even the Soul, who is a greater Interpreter in man between the Spark and personality, eventually vanishes, and man walks in the "clear light of the day."

Thus meditation puts an end to all dreams, and man faces reality as he awakens on higher levels and eventually masters the whole field of manifestation. In esoteric writings we are told that "Initiation is essentially penetration into areas of the divine consciousness which are not within the normal field of consciousness of a human being. This initiatory penetration is achieved by disciples through reflective meditation, the development of an interpretive spiritual understanding, plus the use of the trained discriminative mind."

Meditation is not supposed to be a "happy" time. It is labor, a battle, a struggle, a striving to remove obstacles and penetrate into the core of the seed thought.

After meditating for some time upon tangible objects you can choose a sentence or a word of wisdom or truth, and dwell on it for a week, a month or even a year. The important achievement is not necessarily what you discover in the seed thought; it is the fact that you are strengthening the "muscles" of your mind and tempering your will. Out of such endeavors will develop two of the greatest characteristics of a disciple: steadfastness and endurance. The purpose of meditation is not only the knowledge gained, but rather the organization and transfiguration of the mind and the expansion of consciousness. This expansion comes first through learning and meditation, and then through contact with the transpersonal Self.

When you discover that your mind is slowing down in the process of penetration, approach your seed thought from another angle, from the viewpoint of a bee, a butterfly, a Christ, a Buddha, a man, a woman or a baby. You will find that your seed thought will then open many doors, the existence of which you were unaware.

Another approach is to meditate on your seed thought as if you were a blind, deaf or clairvoyant person, or as a bodyless entity. Perhaps you may assume that you are a tree, a flower or a chair. View the seed thought from as many different angles as possible. This will enable you to rouse your mind from its inertia and challenge it with a fresh outlook.

Most of us meditate through words. We are mentally speaking while meditating. This is a natural stage, but we must try to think without words, through symbols; then later, we must try to view the seed thought using neither symbols nor words. As you so use and expand your consciousness, words lose their meaning and are replaced by symbols; as you progress in your meditation work, the symbols will disappear and you will enter into the world of true meaning, and then into the world of significance and energy. It is because of such achievement that some great minds, after long years of teaching, suddenly open their horizons to such an extent that all their teachings seem to them as toys or baubles, and they enter into the Inner Silence to absorb and assimilate the unlimited vistas spreading before them in their visions.

Sometimes we become so preoccupied with the overcasting clouds that we forget the sun, which IS. The time will come when we will pass over the clouds of knowledge and will look into *Infinity*. This is the meaning of our fourth viewpoint. We try to find the *source* of our seed thought. As we strive to achieve such expansion, our greatest task is breaking up crystallizations of thought. Crystallized thoughts are the results of a way of thinking from which you are unable to divert your mind. You reject any idea or way of thinking which is opposed to your own ideas or way of thinking. You refuse to view the object or subject from different angles, but stubbornly cling to your own ideas which are limited because of this very refusal. You hold to your thought and say, "This is reality." Another person, viewing it from a different angle may say, "No, this is reality." You may both be right, but you are rejecting the thoughts of each other because of crystallizations.

In one of the Brotherhoods which I visited in the Middle East, an interesting and effective method of dissolving crystallizations was used. The teacher collected eight students from different religious backgrounds and told them to prepare an extensive research report about their own religion. Two buddhist students were to prepare their research on Buddhism, two other students on Christianity, and the others on Islam and Hinduism. When the papers were ready they all had a debate, strongly defending their own religions and trying to minimize the value of the others.

After the debate was over the leader of the Brotherhood called these eight students and gave them another task. This time each team was going to do an extensive research on the religion it attacked the most. The Christian group took Buddhism. The Hindus took Islam, etc. and after six months the papers were ready and the debate began. This continued until each group had a chance to defend and speak about all these four religions. At the end the whole group, and the whole Brotherhood were able to find great similarities and beauties in all the religions, and accepted all of them as their religion.

The age-long conflicts and wars behind religions are based wholly on the existence of crystallizations. It was because of crystallizations that man missed the common denominator of all religions which unites humanity upon that common ground of light, love, beauty, Right Human Relations, Goodwill and contact with the Almighty One, within man and cosmos.

Meditation, as we have said, is a labor, a striving. It is not choosing a subject, for example the word forest, and saying, "How beautiful is the forest! I like the forest." It is not imagining yourself sitting under a tree in the forest, creating happy and beautiful dreams. Meditation is *thinking* and finding what the forest is to you, to a snake, a lion, a bear, a bug, a butterfly, a manufacturer, humanity and to the planet itself. Meditation is a process of winding your mind to enable it to handle its daily labors more efficiently.

Many people aspire to an easy life, but a real disciple chooses a life of labor, a life of striving. Even he likes to face difficulties. Difficulties are either mechanically or consciously created. If you want to improve yourself, you consciously create difficulties and overcome them. For example, you decide not to speak for a whole day and then follow through. Decide to send love to someone whom you dislike intensely or someone you are indifferent to. Tell yourself not to eat certain foods of which you are very fond. By so doing you are consciously putting obstacles on your path, creating conscious difficulties. Through these difficulties you are "winding" yourself, creating more energy and alertness and releasing it in greater usefulness, greater freedom and joy.

Your opportunity to progress commences at the point where you meet your obstacles. Progress is achieved by the steps you take to overcome these obstacles. If you experience no obstacles, difficulties or problems, you are not growing. The Tibetan Master suggests, "If you do not have crises, create them." It is through crises and tensions you grow, not through an easy life.

Those who want to meditate must realize first of all that it is like climbing a mountain. You must climb slowly with great difficulty, risk and danger; but eventually, you will reach the mountain top; you will find and experience more light, more communication and more expansion.

One day Socrates was invited to a wedding. Accompanied by his servant he started for the village some five miles away. As they were passing under some beautiful trees, Socrates paused and said, "You go on now to the wedding and I will follow later." He sat down upon a rock and closed his eyes. The servant walked on, looking back several times, only to see his master still sitting on the rock apparently in deep thought. The servant enjoyed himself at the wedding celebration and in the early morning hours returned to the place where he had left his master. He saw that Socrates was still in deep thought so he seated himself at his master's feet and waited. When dawn came Socrates arose and gave an invocation to the Sun, expressing gratitude for the light that had illuminated his heart. Then he said, "Let us return home."

This is true meditation. Socrates had some troublesome problem on his mind which he wanted to solve. He disciplined his physical, emotional and mental bodies to such a degree that they obeyed him all through the night. We do not know how successful he was in solving the problem, he must have accomplished a great deal during this long meditation period. Twenty five hundred years have passed since his death but his ideas are still part of our culture.

Recording the results of your meditation will help to prevent day dreaming.

You should have a paper and pencil at your side and when you finish meditating, write down the ideas that came to you. How many ideas were there? Suppose you decided to think about the words of Master Morya, "Bless the obstacles through them we grow." Think about this sentence every day for a week. Each day record the results of your meditation, your thinking. How many pages can you write about it?

Usually, on the first day, you will write many thoughts; the second day perhaps a half page; the third day, a sentence or two; on the fourth day you will probably repeat what you have written before or you may tell yourself that you have written everything there is to be written about the subject, that you know everything about it, that there is nothing more to write. This shows how lazy the mind can be; it plays tricks on you; but if you challenge it, if you say, "I want to meditate, to analyze and penetrate, to go deeper into the subject and achieve some results," the mind will obey.

There is a technique by which your meditation will become more effective. As you meditate, close your eyes and visualize a group of very intelligent, inquisitive students before you, asking questions. Using your imagination and visualization, try to give the best possible answers.

Have you ever stopped to think what our questions are and where they originate? Our questions are created by the answers which we have in our deeper mind. If you have a question, the answer is found in the deeper layers of your Soul; It is prodding you to find it. There is an answer to every question because the question is the result of the answer found in your mind. If you ask a question, your Soul will forward to you the answer.

We all have had the experience of carrying problems around in our minds to which we have found no solution. For the first couple of days we meet with no success but perhaps on the third or fourth day, while performing some mundane task, the answer suddenly appears. Where does it come from: It comes from within. The solution to a problem is always there within your reach. When you succeed in "tuning-in" to the highest impressions and ideas, they descend into your mind; you become a source of inspiration, of creativity because through meditation you can open the Chalice.

A beautiful story is told of Michelangelo. He and his friends were passing by a huge rock on their way to some festive occasion. Suddenly Michelangelo stopped in front of the rock and stood gazing up at the great, rough stone.

"Why are you stopping? Come, we are late," called one of his companions.

"Go on without me," said Michelangelo. "Leave me here for a while. I am seeing in this great rock a beautiful angel." Realizing that some inspiration had come to their friend, they left him alone by the rock. He began to meditate upon how the rock could be changed into an angel, into a harmonious form which would inspire people. Some time later his friends again passed by the rock and saw that it had, indeed, become a thing of great beauty; it had been changed into a beautiful angel for all who passed by to behold and enjoy.

Through meditation, the "rock" or dark charcoal of the personality, slowly becomes radioactive fire. Meditation changes the personality, charges it with energy, opens greater vision and gradually transforms our physical, emotional and mental vehicles. It helps man direct his own life.

If you observe yourself objectively, you will find that you are not the master of your physical body. Perhaps eighty percent of the earth's population is under the control of the physical body. Some people are controlled by their emotional body, others by an automatic, mechanical thinking which is simply reaction.

Very often we are controlled by thoughts. For example, suppose you have a great fear in your mind. You try, but you are unable to cast it out. It is affecting you in many ways. You are controlled by it. Can you tell yourself that thoughts are not the real "you," and put them out of your mind? If you can do this, you are controlling your mind, your mental nature.

The night before his death, Socrates knew that he was to drink the poison the following morning. On his last evening he gathered his disciples around him and spoke of immortality until dawn. His disciples offered to help him escape but he declined. The idea of dying, the idea of death never entered his mind because he would not allow it to do so. He had control of his mental nature.

Pause for a half hour and observe your mind. You will find that thousands of thoughts are coming and going, criss-crossing and mingling with each other. These thoughts are not originating in your mind, they are coming from the outside and putting your mind into action. Some of these thoughts you welcome and when you identify with them you think that they are your own thoughts. Meditation helps you to stop being a mechanical person; it enables you, instead, to become self-actualized, self-controlled. You become your own master. Your physical, emotional and mental vehicles do not control you; you control them.

To begin a meditation it is necessary to coordinate the mental plane, a very mysterious realm. It is a sphere of light, and in this sphere are billions of tiny atoms darting about. These tiny atoms are of seven hues of yellow color, each representing one level of the mental plane, but the atoms with their different colors are intermingled.

Imagine that these atoms are gradually forming geometric patterns, creating a symphony of color on the mental plane. At the highest point is the magnificent form of a lotus, acting as the inspiration point of this great symphony of color and radiation. Meditation organizes the mental sphere into this living color symphony in which each hue is sensitive to impressions. Meditation then unfolds the bud of the chalice, making it a radioactive, fiery lotus which transmits light, love and power from the Solar Angel to the personality.

In meditation our purpose is not to calm the mind or put it to sleep. On the contrary, we refine this instrument to such a degree that it will be able to translate ideas, to formulate them, making them useful in our daily life. This is meditation. We do not want to be mystics who go to the mountains and sit and dream for thirty years. In our present-day world we need greater mental instruments, greater "machines" illumined with the light, minds that are capable of formulating all those truths, those sciences which will serve to uplift our entire civilization, and solve our many problems.

In the past, meditation has been grossly misunderstood by most people. They thought that it was a dream process carried on by lazy people or dreamers. Actually, meditation is very hard mental work. After the mental body is completely sublimated, you will not stop there; you will then endeavor to penetrate the intuitional level. It is impossible, however to function upon the intuitional plane without completely building and totally purifying your mental atoms. If you should pass for a short time to the intuitional plane without building the mental plane, the ideas that come to your mental level will be mistranslated; and they will cause much trouble, sadness, depression, illness and many complications.

Meditation is extremely dangerous if it is not handled as a scientific course of study, because you are literally playing with fire, with power, with energy.

If you are unable to align your physical, emotional and mental bodies, and put them under the light of your Inner Guide, the Soul, you can run into danger. For example, if you do not align your emotional vehicle, or mental vehicle, entities may possess one of them and split your personality, or the ideas and thoughts that are coming from higher levels can be so distorted that they become a big source of confusion in your life, and channel undesired force to your various centers.

To avoid such danger you must learn the art of alignment, and have a private place to be used only by you for your meditation. A candle and incense will help to purify the atmosphere and a loose-fitting robe, worn only for your meditation, is desirable. By always doing your meditation, your thinking, here in this special place, you slowly create a magnetic atmosphere; you build a beautiful ''temple'' with your elevated thoughts, with your inspiration, with your prayers and invocations.

If at times you are distressed or feeling depressed, enter into your own meditation place and sit for a few minutes. You will immediately feel the change. The energy there will uplift you, and charge you.

We must try to organize our lives in such a way that we will be able to meditate at five o'clock every morning. The next best hour is nine A.M. or it may be done at sunset. Whatever time you choose at your convenience, try to keep the same hour each day. In so doing you will discipline your physical, emotional and mental natures and create a rhythm and harmony between you and the higher spheres with which you are trying to fuse.

The duration of meditation must be limited to fifteen minutes for the first three years. It can be very dangerous if the time factor is not considered. The wrong kind of meditation carried on for twenty or thirty minutes can destroy your nervous system, your mind, or cause mental illness; but a ten to fifteen-minute meditation performed with knowledge of the art becomes a means of transfiguration for you. The brain cells, the head glands, should not receive undue pressure through meditation; they must gradually become accustomed to the pressure and heat that it creates. Pressure-producing meditation eventually brings on fatigue, nervousness, indigestion, pains in the head, eyes or ears.

To avoid all these problems, use caution. Move slowly but safely, because the success of meditation is not dependent upon time involved. If you touch *Reality* for one second, you have accomplished much. In the higher mind things are not measured by time. There is no time; there is only eternity and in one moment you can be inspired with a tremendous vision, lofty ideas and insight. People who have been meditating for ten years or more, may safely lengthen their meditation time, but the beginner must proceed with caution.[2]

Another factor to be considered concerning meditation is breathing. Before

2. Read *The Science of Meditation* by H. Saraydarian, chap. 26.

you start your meditation, check your breathing and make it calm, deep and rhythmical. Breathing exercises should not be practiced unless they are given and supervised by a Master. Such exercises can bring on many physical problems if done without proper knowledge. They can open a channel between the etheric, physical and astral bodies, and if you are not equipped with strong health, good mechanisms and the correct technique of meditation, you may become the victim of evil forces. Before meditation, simply sit quietly and gently regulate your inhalation and exhalation, making it deep and serene.

Sleep is also an important consideration in regard to meditation. We must have at least six hours of sleep before we meditate. Sleep regenerates our etheric body and nervous system and gives us an opportunity to have some communication with the Teachers of the inner world.

After we leave our bodies in sleep, we are attracted to those spheres where the subject of our interest is taught by those men and women who are able to function consciously in their mental bodies and teach those who are ready for such instruction. Although, we seldom remember it the impression remains with us, and in our daily life we try to live by what we have learned.

After we have succeeded in building the rainbow bridge, we will have achieved continuity of consciousness which will enable us to remember all that happens to us during sleep on higher planes.

Another important point is our food. Food has a cleansing influence on our feeling and thinking. It is suggested that we eat mostly vegetables, fruits and nuts. There are three kinds of food:

1. Those which cause inertia in your system.
2. Those which cause motion and excitement in your system.
3. Those which give rhythm, health, joy and strength.

Discover from your own experience which foods will give your system rhythm, health and joy.

We must also consider sex. Those who want to advance on the spiritual path should not waste their energies, but should use them for creative purposes. As related to meditation, we should not meditate immediately after making love. It is essential that we have at least six hours of sleep after the act before meditating. If we do not observe this rule, we can eventually create very bad effects in our physical bodies.

The Masters of the Wisdom strongly emphasize the fact that drugs, tobacco and alcohol are enemies of our spiritual progress and of the health of our whole system. Their use will create obsessions, cause cracks in our auras, damage our brains and render us unable to receive great and true inspirations from the core of our essence. When the brain is loaded with poison, it cannot clearly transmit messages coming from the mind and from higher sources.

Before we can engage in successful meditation, we must learn how to concentrate. We must be able to focus the ray of our minds so firmly upon an object that we cannot be distracted by any other object or idea. We should be able to look at an object for ten or fifteen minutes with observing and penetrating eyes. Many exercises to improve our power of concentration are given in detail in *The Science of Meditation*, pages 71-78.

Concentration is followed by meditation and meditation is followed by contemplation, illumination and inspiration.

Contemplation occurs at that moment when the developing human soul gradually tunes himself in with the light of the Inner Guide and begins to see the great depth, beauty and joy that lies beyond his daily reach. Here he learns great wisdom, experiences great revelations and achieves great insight. He is in touch with the plans and visions of the Inner Thinker. Greater horizons of Cosmos come before his eyes and he sees at-one-ment with the Soul Who is "an Initiate of all degrees." This is not a dream state. On the contrary, it is a state of awakening to realities beyond human conception. All these realities are reflected upon the higher mind and passed to the lower mind for necessary formulation and use. Through contemplation rare beauties are brought into expression. If the mind is not developed and purified by true meditation, the expression of these beauties will be distorted. However, if the mind has the necessary purification, discipline and a clear line of communication with the higher mind, these beauties will express themselves in their full glory. We are told that contemplation leads to illumination.

Illumination is the moment of seeing yourself as you are in relation to eternity. You become aware of the role you are going to play in the plan of the Hierarchy. Illumination is like a great magnet, a whirlpool of energy, which holds you in a sphere of great sacrifice and labor; all difficulties on your path increase your courage, your fire and your glory. You are no longer the slave of your glamors, illusions and vanities. You know yourself, you know the Path, you know the goal and you are ready to labor as you walk toward that goal.

Inspiration is the direction that you receive from your Inner Guide. Inspiration produces energy and drive within an enlightened person. You are caught in a whirlpool of mighty energy which tries to find expression through you. The success of such expression will depend on the level upon which you stand as an unfolding individual. For an inspired person there exist no obstacles or hindrances which cannot be annihilated. Inspiration makes you act, speak and think in harmony with the great Plan and the Purpose behind the Plan. It also comes from your Inner Core, the Monad, the Spark, who encourages you to live a life of great beauty and sacrifice. After you have achieved these stages, you may be *consciously* inspired by a Great Being for greater service to humanity.

The man who travels his own road of evolution will eventually work on these five steps of concentration, meditation, contemplation, illumination and inspiration to achieve self mastery.

Aspiration is different than inspiration; it is a process of orientation towards a goal. When you are caught in a magnetic field of great beauty and try to reach it, we say that you are aspiring. Aspiration can be a lower response to a higher inspiration. Aspiration is a form of invocation and inspiration is a form of evocation.

There are people who are members of many organizations, who study many kinds of teaching but in the end find themselves totally confused. It is wiser to remain in one study group than to be continually changing from one to·another. Those who synthesize the teaching can really help us to see the unity behind the diversity. The direction you take must originate from within you, from your experience and intuition, and these are developed through meditation and service. Master Morya, speaking of the Teaching says,

"So many distortions, so many inaccuracies, have been admitted into the teaching. Verily, each purification is great service. Each striving to renew the truth, as it has been given to humanity, is fiery *service*."[3]

Those who wander from one teacher to another have not yet acquired the inner compass, and are not directed toward the true Teaching. They will experience much suffering before they reach the right direction and the true Teaching. Meditation helps such people to build within themselves a *sense of direction* and *clear thinking*. Clear thinking produces the faculty of insight. Those who meditate through the four viewpoints eventually reach the state of clear thinking, which leads them in the right direction on any level.

Meditation is an active thinking process. Deep in our hearts we know the truth, the beauty, the goodness. Meditation is the labor we perform to touch these treasures, to intelligently bring them into our daily life and thus make our life an expression of truth, beauty and goodness. This is creative thinking; this is true meditation.

What are some of the signs of successful meditation?

We can say that one of the signs is growing common sense, a balanced way of living, an increasing sense of unity, a thirst to know and to be, a deepening sense of responsibility.

With all these you will have a sense of transiency. This will help you to develop conscious and healthy detachment from many kinds of objects, people, and ideas. Things will appear to you in their inner values, and the things that you were adoring and cherishing deeply will often disappear from the field of your love.

One of the greatest signs of successful meditation is an increasing urge to serve and radiate joy and courage, and to stand on your own feet and be a self-actualized person.

Meditation is the process of touching or contacting the power house, or treasure house within you. As you touch that center of power and glory, your whole physical, emotional and mental vehicles are charged with power and joy. Our physical and mental vehicles function through the energy coming from our Soul, or from the Inner Guide, and this energy is called psychic energy.

Psychic energy is the true electrical energy for the whole man. Even prana or other energies are not assimilated into our threefold personality, if we lack psychic energy. Psychic energy increases and circulates more systematically through our three systems, when proper meditation is done and proper service is rendered as a result of right meditation. It is this psychic energy which heals the body, purifies the emotional system and organizes and transmutes the whole mental vehicle. As a result of this you have greater control upon your physical body, greater control upon your emotional reaction and greater control upon your mental mechanism.

In most of the people thought-forms, thought-waves, or mental impressions of other minds control their minds, and they call this kind of mental activity,

3. Agni Yoga Society, *Fiery World*, vol. III, p. 125.

"thinking." Through right meditation this can be overcome and man can use his mind according to his needs and plans without being the slave of thought-waves that run wild in the fields of his mind.

Another great sign of successful meditation is an urge toward more simplification. When a man does right meditation for many years, you see a greater simplicity in all his expressions; even the most complicated matters are presented by him in most simple stories, symbols or words.

We must not imagine that all these gifts will be ours in a very short time. There are other things that may happen. For example, lots of cleansing must take place in our vehicles, before we see a steady rise of beauties in our nature. Sometimes these cleansing problems are painful, discouraging and tiresome but through all clouds of such a cleansing process, the Sun is sensed and its love and light is felt.

Meditation relates you directly to God. It is a process of transforming yourself into God. You are becoming a conscious part of Him, because in meditation you are thinking about the laws of Cosmos. You are freeing your consciousness from the slavery of your physical, emotional and mental environment. You are cooperating with the Creator; transforming the substance of the mind, of emotions, of space. You are coming to the Light and in that Light you are seeing the Great Consciousness Who is controlling all of Cosmos; you are approaching Him. You are changing, becoming Yourself; and if you are becoming Yourself, you are becoming Him, for He is One in all of us. You are a tiny Spark of Him and when you touch your real Essence you are reaching out and touching Him.

CHAPTER 15

ILLUMINATION

Meditation is the technique for illumination; illumination is the result of persistent service and meditation in the light-of the Soul.

Illumination is a process of awakening. For example, one slowly awakens in a dark room. A very faint light appears which gradually increases as the sun rises. At first he can only see 1% of his surroundings, then 10-15%, later 80-90%, and eventually he sees *things as they really are*.

It is not easy "to see things as they really are." Gradual illumination not only helps us to see things as they are in outer form, but also their etheric counterpart, their emotional and mental natures, their quality, purpose and cause, and their relationship to existence as a whole.

Illumination not only clarifies things as they are on the physical plane, but also as they are on the astral and mental planes, and in their archetypal state. Illumination is a gradual process of entering into higher states of consciousness; higher states of awareness; and communication from these higher planes with the field of existence. Many people are confused about the true meaning of enlightenment because they are looking at the subject from the viewpoint of intellectual understanding. Enlightenment can be known through the process of illumination, as the nature of the waking state can only be known after one emerges from sleep.

The Enlightenment is a gradual process of awakening to the reality of a person's true Self. Through intelligent observation he becomes aware of his nature, emotions and mental state; he realizes what he is able to do and what cannot be accomplished by him. All his miseries and weaknesses become apparent and he wants to eliminate them. He senses a latent possibility in himself which, if allowed to develop, will enable him to become his own master.

Illumination is not only seeing things as they exist on different levels, but also relating the parts to the greater whole. This stage reveals also the needs of the parts in the whole picture and the steps required to meet these needs. An enlightened mechanic, for instance, not only owns a good machine shop but knows how to use his machines in order to meet the needs of others. The willingness to help grows within him in proportion to the increase of light within him. On the one hand, the human being strives to increase his light by service and meditation; on the other, he responds to a higher pressure coming from Space which brings about a slow awakening. Actually the process of enlightenment has three steps.

At the first step the mental permanent atom irradiates the mental plane as a whole and fuses it with its light. This process affects the emotional plane and cleanses it from age-long glamors and makes it a pure channel of intuitional love.

It is in this degree of enlightenment that the initiate comes in contact with the plan of his Soul. He becomes conscious of all possibilities in his life, he sees his karmic hindrances, the right way, and the right place to serve.

On the second degree of enlightenment the light of the intuition pours down to the whole mental plane and reveals the plan for humanity and the plan of all

75

kingdoms of nature. The initiate finds his position within the greater plan and adjusts all his activities according to this revelation.

The plan is built by the intuitional substance, and as this substantial energy or fire increases within the mental plane, the deeper layers of the plan unfold gradually in his consciousness.

This step reveals the greater whole of the Hierarchical activities, and enormously increases the flow of love energy which changes into energy of magnetism and attraction.

On the third step of enlightenment, the energy of the atmic plane pours down to the mental plane, and charges it with the energy of the will. The mental activities express powerful will and the man now has the energy he needs to carry into fulfillment the revelations that were given to him in the course of his enlightenment. The atmic energy is often called the ''progressing light'' which carries the initiate into fields of great service and responsibilities.

This energy is accumulated in the Soul, burns age-long maya and releases man into intense spiritual service.

This whole process of the enlightenment takes many years or incarnations.

The third initiation, the Initiation of enlightenment, mentioned in the life of Buddha and Jesus, is the final Seal of the achievement of the three phases of the path of enlightenment.

The Zodiac is a great Life which has twelve signs each of which is like a petal of a lotus. Through these twelve centers, this Life radiates its influence to Space and strives for better communication with the greater whole. The Zodiac is a center in Space exercising a tremendous pressure for expansion of consciousness, which releases the Spirit throughout Space to all forms and beings to be found within its sphere of influence. This great Lotus also has a cosmic drive to expand within itself and reach towards greater Infinity. Age by age its petals are unfolding, radiating greater energy, with an increasing variety of colors, music and beauty.

May we dare to say that the Life ensouling the Zodiac as a whole is on the path of Cosmic Illumination, seeking to see things as they are in a Cosmic sense, in relation to Infinity? This urge is reflected in man who also has a little nucleus or bud of light within his mental sphere which gradually unfolds to form a twelve-petaled Lotus. As it unfolds, this bud radiates greater light as its response to that great Life increases, and greater striving, sacrifice and service become apparent. As the petals unfold they exercise greater pressure for illumination on the cells and atoms of the physical, etheric, emotional and mental vehicles; these become aligned and integrated and gradually release their latent light which blends with the light radiating from the center of the petals.

As this process of illumination progresses, the mental mirror of the man becomes purer and purer, until it reflects the *beauties* from the Intuitional plane enabling man to see the star of his eternal path, his eternal goal. For a moment he identifies himself with the glory of that *star*, that Future, and the inspiration and the charge that he gains from this experience never fades but becomes an unceasing source of energy giving him the courage to strive for the realization of his destiny: Ever-expanding beauty, love and service in the path of his increasingly creative life.

The Illumination or unfoldment of the Zodiac, the Solar System, the planet and the man can eventually become synchronized as their inner life becomes more sensitive to the greater call, and the form refines and expresses that call. One wonders if the Zodiacal Life itself is not listening for the call emitted by a Cosmic Magnet, acting as a shining guide on the higher planes of Infinity.

Man on his own level reflects all that takes place in Cosmos, and his unfoldment and illumination are *predestined* by the great Lives in whose bodies we are acting as little cells. In ancient Greek mythology this drama of illumination and mastery is symbolized by the labours of Hercules. The twelve labours, each represented in a sign of the Universal Zodiac are the twelve principal responses of the human soul to the urge of enlightenment emanating from that Central Life. Each labour carried the unfoldment process a little farther, until the lotus in the human being came into full bloom. We can say that the human soul after such an unfoldment is in harmony in lower octaves with the symphony of that Great Life.

Man's lotus has twelve petals, divided as follows: Three knowledge petals, three love petals, and three sacrificial petals. The innermost three petals are the dynamic sources of these outer three tiers of petals.

The inner Hercules, the unfolding human soul on its journey, reaches a point where it slowly responds to the great urge of enlightenment, and gradually enters into the rhythm of the Enlightenment.

First his three knowledge petals are unfolded, bestowing on him enlightenment on physical, emotional and mental realms. Then his love petals begin to unfold, giving him greater realization of love in these realms. Finally his sacrificial petals are unfolded, making him a radioactive beacon for a great span of time. This gradual unfoldment brings about increasing radiation of light, deeper and greater contact with existence and better expression of the divinity within man.

It is interesting to note that in the Zodiac itself, we have three crosses. They are called

Mutable Cross
Fixed Cross
Cardinal Cross

Each cross is comprised of four signs, with four constellations.

The signs of the Mutable Cross correspond to the Knowledge petals.[1]

The signs of the Fixed Cross correspond to the Love petals.[2]

And the signs of the Cardinal Cross correspond to the Sacrificial petals.[3]

On the human level when the first petal begins to unfold, a great expansion of consciousness occurs. We see that our physical bodies are not us. We study the bodies more closely and we take better care of them.

When the second petal starts to unfold, our consciousness penetrates a little further into the emotional nature of our beings, and we gradually feel that we are

1. Gemini, Virgo, Sagitarrius, Pisces.
2. Taurus, Leo, Scorpio, Aquarius.
3. Aries, Cancer, Libra, Capricorn.

not our emotions. We do not have control over our emotions, but we start to see the games our emotions are playing through the spheres of our sensitive bodies. We still do not have control over them, though we see the bodies as they function.

These first two petals bestow on us rare knowledge about our physical and emotional bodies and about the nature of other people. We do not identify others with their physical bodies and urges, nor with their emotions. We can see these people acting through their bodies, but also see that they are not their physical and emotional bodies, and we become more patient and understanding of them. We come to know other people in the same degree that we know ourselves.

The unfolding of the third petal brings us a greater expansion of consciousness. In this stage we see that our minds are instruments being used by us. We start to learn how the mind functions. The first thing we realize is that it functions like a machine mainly controlled by other minds, thoughts and external influences. We realize also that we cannot get away from it.

A story is told about Socrates. He was talking with a man, trying to disprove his ideas about a certain subject. Eventually the man came to realize that he was in error, but the shock of the realization cost him his life.

Where our opinions, thoughts and knowledge are concerned, we are vulnerable when someone proves that they are without foundation and incorrect. At this stage of unfoldment, fanaticism is a crystalization. When, by your supremacy you force yourself on others as they permit this, you feel elated; however, should they reject you, you feel hatred towards them. Thus you become a slave-producing machine. But once your fanaticism is destroyed, you lose your desire to live. This stage is still limited by the extent of our observation; the true enlightenment will start with the unfoldment of the next petal.

The fourth petal, technically called the first Love petal, brings a greater enlightenment as it unfolds in the physical, etheric bodies. This brings detachment from the physical plane. We not only realize that the physical body is not us, but we now have knowledge and energy to control it in the highest degree.

At this stage our physical habits slowly fade away. Physical urges and drives are controlled and inertia is eliminated. The body becomes energetic, active, endurable and able to support the greater strain and stress under which the unfolding disciple must operate. When this stage reaches a high degree of stability, man takes the *First Initiation of Threshold*, as it is called in the Ancient Wisdom.

Initiations are the culmination of certain degrees of control and enlightenment. Man's light increases gradually and when it reaches a certain point of tensity, he breaks through his former ring of consciousness and enters into a greater field of consciousness, awareness and actualization.

After a person takes the first initiation, his orientation leads him towards higher values, which may demonstrate to himself and others that he is living under higher spiritual values. Eventually his fifth petal begins to open, at which time he experiences a steadily growing control over his emotional body, emotional reactions and negativity. Slowly his emotional nature changes into an all-giving love. When a person's emotional nature is pure and controlled, he feels a tremendous freedom from self-made prisons; he has become a wellspring of love and beauty.

It is well to mention that no petal opens individually without causing stimulation or slight unfoldment in others.

The next step is the unfolding of the sixth petal of the lotus which is the third Love petal. As it unfolds, the emotional body passes through higher transformations; the increasing light of the mental plane pours down and eventually eliminates all glamors as the seventh petal opens and the nature of man becomes all dedication, all-giving love, harmlessness and adoration.

When the eighth petal is fully open, man enters into the second expansion of consciousness which is the culmination of the purification process of the astral body. The astral body becomes a mirror which reflects the light shining in his higher planes.

As the ninth petal opens, the unfolding human soul gains control over his mental nature. The mental body becomes a shining light, under the direction and inspiration of the human soul. When the mind is controlled, man becomes successful in his social and spiritual fields, his health improves; he acquires greater peace, greater ability to assimilate higher concepts, and closer contact with the inner Thinker. As the light on the mental plane increases, age-long accumulations of painful experiences within his lower mind gradually come to the surface and are washed away. This provides a great release for his physical body, brain, and emotional nature, which have been indirectly responding to an accumulation of powerful experiences and hypnotic suggestions.

At the third Initiation the disciple recapitulates his labor upon the sixth, seventh and eighth petals and his goal becomes the opening of the ninth petal. The third Initiation is always related to light, as in the Transfiguration of Jesus and the Enlightenment of Buddha. Let us not forget that petals seven, eight and nine are called the Sacrificial petals and after the opening of the ninth petal, man becomes a living sacrifice who demonstrates an all-giving nature and attunement with the highest good for all humanity.

At the Fourth Initiation the three innermost petals open. When they are in process of opening fully, we say that man is on the path of great renunciation. When these three innermost petals reach their ultimate unfoldment, the central fire is released and burns away the chalice—and man enters the path of Mastership.[4]

It is interesting to note that as the petals unfold, a man's life enters into closer relationship with the purpose of the Great Life and with the plan through which that purpose is carried out. The ascending man becomes the expression of Goodness, Beauty and Truth, as a budding violinist eventually perfects his style and becomes a part of the orchestra.

This is the Labor of Hercules; the labor of each striving human soul. Hercules worked very hard. In the first four labors he developed and unfolded the Knowledge petals; in the next four labors his Love petals opened; and eventually in his last four labors he developed his Sacrificial petals and advanced from the Path of Initiation to the Path of Mastership.

These petals exist within man's aura, but the disciple does not concentrate on them, nor does he practice various exercises and so-called meditations to speed their unfoldment. They naturally and safely open as a result of his sacrificial service, discipline of life, striving towards purity and expansion of consciousness and love. The sacrificial service rendered for all humanity is the shortest path of

---

4. Read *The Science of Meditation* by H. Saraydarian, pp. 190-191.

achievement. Practicing the wrong kinds of meditations, postures and breathing exercises to speed the petals in their unfoldment may result in dire consequences to one's health and sanity.

As man responds to the call of the greater life with "self-forgetfulness, harmlessness, and right speech," the petals open and radiate their blissful luminescence and man eventually becomes a light shining upon the mountain top. Some flowers open their petals as the sun appears on the horizon, and some move their petals to follow the sun, becoming open chalices to be filled with the life-giving rays of the Sun. This is also true of man. As he faces the Highest and opens himself to the inspiration and impressions coming from the Highest, he unfolds and radiates as he devotes his life to meditation and service.

When Lord Buddha spoke about the Wheel of Incarnations, he referred to the Wheel of the Zodiac, within the signs of which man reincarnates continuously until he awakens and turns his life towards the Sun, at which time he travels through the reversed Zodiac and becomes a Hercules. In each sign he will learn important lessons, realize and express greater love, and demonstrate a greater willingness to sacrifice.

As man unfolds, the greater Zodiac finds a purer channel by which He may reach the lower kingdoms and create a greater symphony in the Cosmos. It is on this reversed path, the path of Conscious Evolution, that a man meets his inner Guide and, later, his Master.

It is interesting to note that the petals of the Lotus are formed by little lives on the path of evolution and enlightenment. They are striving to unfold as a unit and as a whole, as they advance on their path to perfection.

The Lotus or the Chalice of the Planetary or Solar Logos is formed by great Masters, Lives or Entities of high order. Because the "atoms" of Their chalices are on a higher level of evolution, Their awareness is enhanced. So will man have greater conscious awareness and control as the petals open and the "lives" of the petals unfold and proceed on the path of evolution.

After the chalice has been burned away, it is replaced by the higher counterpart of the chalice, the Spiritual Triad. Man's awareness works within the Spiritual Triad and his personality reflects the light in its purest form.

The story of enlightenment or illumination is the story of the expansion of consciousness and awareness. An enlightened man has a broader understanding of matter, energy, space and time, more intensified control over them and a greater sense of responsibility in his handling of them.

In Sanskrit we find the word "Budhi," meaning discernment of good from evil, or discrimination between right and wrong. It refers also to divine conscience, to pure love and to straight knowledge. In the West we use the word "intuition" as a synonym of the word "Budhi." We also have the word *Buddha*, the Enlightened One, the One who entered into the Light of Budhi—Intuition. The word "Buddha" comes from the root "Budh" which means to *see*, to perceive, to know, to awake, to recover consciousness. Thus each Buddha is an enlightened being awakened to the realities of great life, one who has much knowledge and love to give to the cause of the liberation of humanity. Hence a Buddha is the embodiment of pure Wisdom.

Evolution is a total process. No one is isolated on his path of evolution. Each form tries to enter into the main stream of Cosmic evolution, at first unconsciously, later in full consciousness. As each life increases its own light, it increases the light of others.

Illumination is a gradual process of transmutation, transformation and transfiguration. In the life stories of many mystics we find references to sudden enlightenment, as when lightning pierces the dark sky, revealing great beauties, laws, and parts of the plan and purpose of life. The cause of such enlightenment may be any of the following:

1. Physical shocks which permit the accumulating light to strike the brain and nervous system.
2. Emotional shocks, causing clearance of some of the glamors from the emotional body.
3. Mental shocks, causing clearance of the illusions in the mental sphere to some degree.
4. Artificial means, such as the use of drugs, breathing exercises and chanting.

Through such means light flashes from the intuitional plane bringing revelations which can be of long or short duration, depending on the receptivity of the individual and the condition of the bodies in which he lives. Such illuminations often produce a strong spirit of striving toward greater realizations. Sometimes it leads to greater dedication and service. However, if the light flashes upon a polluted nature, it leads the subject into depression and negativity, or into strong mental illusions and glamors which may produce false prophets, masters and christs. Individuals and groups degenerate. Religious organizations become contaminated with separativeness, hatred and crime when they evoke so much energy for which they are unprepared. We can see such consequences when certain churches become open stages upon which the followers are trying to play and demonstrate their vanities, prides, hatreds, urges, jealousies, and personal interests.

When the vehicles of man are not purified with special diet, rest, pure air and water; when the motives are not for the good of the whole; the energy which descends creates greater glamor and illusions resulting in an abundance of self-deceived individuals in the fields of religion, politics, etc.

The energies of light can be creative, healing and uplifting when the mental nature is not only purified, but developed to a high degree enabling the aspirant to understand and translate the messages transmitted by the energies of light from higher planes. When the mind is not unfolded but man reacts to these energies with a purely emotional nature, then mystics are produced with all their impractical demonstrations. This mystical attitude becomes fanaticism when the light descends into an undeveloped mind.

The important point to be emphasized here is that in gradual illumination, through the activity of the petals, the bodies are refined, purified and transformed to such a degree that glamors and illusions are destroyed and the nature of the man is enabled to reflect the light without distortion. This is not the case when direct impact of the intuitional light on the lower bodies is brought about through shocks and artificial means. Illumination is a steadily-running fountain of inspiration and creativity while the petals are in the process of unfolding. If the illumination is the result of shocks and artificial means, it may produce some passing (temporary) creativity. Man is inspired for a short period of time, he becomes creative in certain ways, but eventually the source of his inspiration dries up. This happens when he has a fairly well-balanced mind and emotional body without an unfolding Lotus.

True enlightenment starts with the third Initiation when the subject has become purified in his motives, freed from his heavy karma, and can consciously contact his inner Guardian and do His will. Illumination is a process of transmutation of the atoms comprising our bodies, the result of the innate light of each atom in response to the light radiating from the petals of the lotus, and the result of the downpouring light from buddhic and atmic planes through the unfolding petals. Such an illumination eventually leads the disciple to the mount of transfiguration.

Illumination proceeds by steps. The first step is an intense sincerity and willingness to face oneself, which may be called self observation. The second step is meditation or discipline of the mind in the light of the Soul. The third step is turning the rays of the mind upon the glamors, and working towards their dissipation. The fourth step is devoting oneself to a selfless service. The fifth step is striving to eliminate the illusions on the mental plane. The sixth step is the appearance of the light in the head which is the result of the interpenetration of the fields of energy emanating from the pineal gland and pituitary body. Actually, the combining of these two fields is the result of increased energy produced by the unfolding petals of the lotus. The seventh step is the changing of the light into the third eye. **The third eye is the birth of the human soul.** The above-mentioned glands act as father and mother, and the relationship between them gives birth to the child, the unfolding human *soul*.

Man awakens when the third eye is opened and he must now gradually begin to use it to enable him to achieve perfection. It is an instrument over which he must have perfect control. Now he has been born as a soul and must go forward towards maturity on higher planes.

In relation to the chalice, or the twelve-petaled lotus, the third eye is the central core of the lotus. The petals may be likened to veils obscuring the central fire, or the central core. As they open, petal by petal, the core comes into closer contact with the planes of existence, and when nine petals have been fully opened, we see the eye as in a mist, formed by the innermost three petals. This formation first appears as a focus of light on the mirror of the mental plane, a mirror which is formed by the electromagnetic field consisting of the radiating petals, four mental centers, and by the two radiating glands. First it reflects on the purified mental plane, then on the etheric, and finally on the magnetic field of the pineal and pituitary glands. As the innermost petals unfold, the formation of the eye reaches perfection. After the fourth Initiation has been attained the eye shines in all its beauty and the Initiate can use it as an instrument of communication and construction or destruction, as about the destiny of the atoms or the lives of the chalice, while the chalice was in process of burning, we can say that:

The word burning is understood esoterically as a process of transmutation through fire. At the time of burning the atoms or lives are not destroyed but are scattered to build different formations on various levels. Only the form of the chalice is dissipated and vanished. In this case the burning of the chalice is a process of initiation, a transmutation for all atoms or lives composing the various petals. Thus they are released from the responsibility or duty in forming a chalice and serving specific purposes, and now are ready to be useful for other tasks of their own and others.

Also we must remember that the atoms or lives of each petal have different degrees of evolution according to their roles in the chalice.

At the fifth Initiation, the Initiate identifies with the eye; He becomes the eye itself. Let us not forget that **the soul is the eye of the monad**.

It must be emphasized here that we are not speaking about etheric, or astral vision. This may or may not function before the opening of the third eye.

Some students confuse the third eye with the ajna center, when in deep meditation they begin to see a focussed light with winged radiations. The ajna center is composed of a central focus of light with two wings each having 48 petals, glowing with the colors of rose, yellow, blue and purple. This phenomena can become visible as a result of overstressed mental activity and strong aspiration. Most reports of seeing the third eye actually refer to the ajna center.

One of my friends who was writing a book about the third eye, assuming that some of his experiences were the process of opening the third eye, wrote to me asking permission to quote some excerpts from my book ''The Science of Meditation.'' When I received his booklet, I was surprised to find a total distortion of my meaning in one of his paragraphs. I wrote and asked him to let me know the page of the quotation, and I added: ''please check if your paraphrasing is correct.'' He replied giving the page and the paragraph and his paraphrasing.

Next day he sent another letter with some excuses for his distortion of the paragraph and gave a new version of his paraphrasing. It was still wrong. I tried to explain its meaning to him, and ended with the following words: — ''The third eye when it functions, not only your inner vision expands and revelations occur, but also on the physical and actual world you see things as they are, and you do not read things through your own thoughts and associations, but see the actual meanings of the words and phrases.

''If this is not the case, all your 'third-eye' experiences are experiences of astral reflections of the activities of the centers.''

Some writers consider the state of illumination ''cosmic consciousness.'' This is a very tempting term but in my opinion, no man has reached cosmic consciousness at the time of transfiguration or enlightenment or the third initiation. Not even our Solar Logos has yet reached full Cosmic Consciousness, though His Consciousness penetrates every form, every atom, every cell in the Solar System. Let us not forget that our Solar Logos is still an aspirant into the mysteries of our Galaxy....

I wonder how a man could achieve ''Cosmic Consciousness'' before becoming an initiate into the Hierarchy of this small planet! Everything written or said by the enlightened ones is a shining light for humanity, but let us not forget that these are kindergarten teachings by comparison with the teachings given on Logoic levels. Let us not lose our humility or our sense of proportion.

''Illumination'' when it is premature and the result of over-stimulation by any external aid, such as breathing exercises, chanting, drugs, obsession or special meditation to force open psychic centers, can have fatal consequences over the three-fold vehicles of the personality.

Even the period of illumination, if extended beyond the capacity of the given mechanism, can eventually debase the mechanism and create dire psychological consequences: depression, negativity and fear being the least of them.

The aspirant on the path must spend a long time preparing his vehicles, building and purifying them to such a degree that the heavy, increasing voltage of enlightenment can only create radioactivity and not degeneration or decay. Premature illumination also brings great complications of the subject's environment, over-stimulating and cracking the vehicles of those whose unfoldment on the spiritual path has been artificially speeded.

True enlightenment can be achieved only by those who have had their physical bodies sanctified since childhood, whose emotional world is a fountain of love and joy, and whose mental sphere is disciplined, balanced, trained in receptivity of higher voltage of ideas and vision, and is highly creative. We must emphasize that through illumination man is not becoming an omniscient being. This is a great illusion on the part of those who speak about attaining Cosmic Consciousness. Illumination, which starts with a spark, gradually expands to become a radiant Sun but the Sun itself is a mere candle in comparison to Infinity.

We have Planetary enlightenment, Solar enlightenment, Cosmic enlightenment...and——beyond.

Let us mention some of the virtues of an enlightened man.

An enlightened man is an optimist. This is not the result of his emotional and mental reactions to his experiences, but a consequence of his insight into the future. The curious thing is that his optimism does not prevent him from seeing the defects and dangers of the moment. He recognizes the wrong motives, or distorted intentions of others. He handles these with love but keeps them harmless. This may be compared to the training of tigers. The trainers love their tigers; they know the dangers involved; but are able to handle both their love and their knowledge of the dangers.

An enlightened man is courageous, daring and fearless but he is not a fool. His courage, daring and fearlessness are the result of his clear vision and understanding of reality. He risks his life only if he is sure that in losing it he will save a greater number of lives or bring greater unfoldment and progress to humanity.

He can move quickly. He forgives but is vigilant and watchful of your next move. He trusts you but does not initiate you into a labor for which you are not ready. He recognizes the defects in your work but keeps you at this work so long as you do not get out of control; thereby giving you a chance to discover your hidden weaknesses and remove them.

An enlightened man has neither friends, favorites, nor enemies; only co-workers. For him the important goal is the plan, and whoever is capable of forwarding the working out of the plan is his co-worker.

An enlightened man is an idealist but he is also a very practical man; he is down-to-earth but soars to great heights. An enlightened man has no fear of death, as he already lives in the eternal, but this does not mean that he is careless of his health and the sanitary conditions of his environment. He is a balanced being with balanced activities and a balanced form of expression. He saves a penny and spends millions. He takes long rests and vacation but labors hard and continuously. He knows how to command and how to obey. He is both a teacher and a student. He knows when to speak and when to keep silent. An enlightened man radiates love, magnetism, blessings, serenity, healing powers.

The presence of an enlightened man is a great blessing. He inspires courage, labor, observation, daring and sacrifice. He enables you to meet yourself. He lets you see not only your vanities, but also your eternal star of the future. Above all, he inspires the spirit of striving, endurance, trust, patience and gratitude.

CHAPTER 16

SOUL-INFUSED PERSONALITY

The need of every disciple is ever to develop a closer and more direct alignment between Soul and personality.[1]

—The Tibetan

The Solar Angel lives on the higher mental levels, radiating light, love and power. Its light-aspect gradually penetrates the physical, etheric, astral and mental atmospheres, as the aspiration of the human soul grows and deepens. At first most of the atoms of the three bodies do not respond to the light-aspect of the Soul. Gradually the sensitivity of these atoms increases and the bodies attract more light of intelligence from the Soul. The increase of this light-energy causes the human soul to integrate the three bodies, forming them into a unit, called personality.

We have been told that for centuries man is not an integrated personality, but a member of the masses. The personality is the physical, emotional and mental man, integrated and formed into one mechanism by the magnetic power of the unfolding human soul. The personality is only the mask of the real man and is generally formed by the process of imitating, and accumulating. Our reaction to life in general helps in its formation. It can manifest any characteristic, color, or expression.

The personality passes through three separate stages of development. In the first stage it is a selfish unit working only for its own individual nature. In the second stage, a conflict begins between the Soul expression and the personality reaction. Most of the time the personality rebels against the silent suggestions of the Soul. In the third stage, the personality yields and gradually fuses with the will of the Soul. Here starts the path of discipleship; the unfolding human soul realizes the part it should play in the great Plan. Eventually the second energy, the love energy, starts to pour into the personality. A faint bridge appears between the man and the Soul. The man starts to feel the touch of the Soul, his aspiration increases, and then the power of the Soul begins to flood the personality. These three energies of the Soul gradually penetrate the whole substance of the three vehicles and fuse with the life of the personality; a transmutation process begins in the vehicles, and man becomes a soul-infused personality. The unfolding human soul and the Solar Angel become fused. The personality now ceases to be a concealing veil or misleading mask. It becomes a truer picture of the inner man, who shines through the physical body as acts of service, through the emotional body as love and compassion, and through the mental body as knowledge and right human relations.

The Solar Angel affects man in seven-year cycles. First, He energizes the physical-etheric man through the life thread anchored in the heart center. Then He starts to affect the emotional life through the ages seven to fourteen and the

---

1. A. A. Bailey, *Discipleship in the New Age*, vol. 1, p. 126.

mental life through the ages fourteen to twenty-one. During these 21 years the Solar Angel charges the bodies or the three vehicles. He barely touches them, which has an organizing effect upon the bodies; they become integrated and prepare for more advanced work in the future.

At age 21, the second touch of appropriation of the etheric body commences; it passes to the emotional body and then to the mental body. This time the touch is stronger and can be very rewarding for the man if, in the previous cycles, his vehicles have been developed and used in higher activities. Theoretically, at age 49 man is mature and if he had been wise enough to unfold and develop himself, he would see the true path and have enough energy and light to enter it in full consciousness. The contact of the Solar Angel with the sleeping human soul liberates it from glamors and illusions, expands its consciousness and develops its sense of reality.

Most actions of the personality are automatic and mechanical. The personality is a stimulus-response apparatus; many of our actions are mechanical responses to physical, emotional and mental stimuli. We have a choice of two ways of responding—the personality way and the Soul way. A great part of our life is controlled by the first, which makes man the victim of his surrounding conditions, events and blind urges of the physical, emotional and mental vehicles. But, as the Soul-light penetrates into the mental layers and awakens the human soul, a transmutation process commences and gradually the mechanical actions of man decrease, and conscious actions increase until the whole mechanism comes under the control of the Soul-consciousness. This process is called Soul-infusion.

Soul-infusion is not easily achieved, it requires continuous hardship and struggle, pain and crisis, service and sacrifice. Age-long habits of the personality do not yield easily, and man passes through great depressions, conflicts and "dark nights." These things come about because the inpouring Soul-light creates friction in the substance of the three worlds. Man passes from one crisis to another until, gradually, rhythmic vibration permeates the three bodies simultaneously. Man has become a Soul-infused entity.

Upon different bodies, Soul-infusion causes diverse effects. In the etheric-physical body it creates a radioactive energy; the physical man is full of energy, which he can control and use beneficially; his senses are very keen; he projects peace, poise, and serenity. In the emotional body, Soul-infusion brings peace and calmness; it generates extreme sensitivity to higher impulses; man's emotions become strong and positive; his imagination becomes extensive and creative; he devotes himself to higher causes and acts enthusiastically. In the mental body, Soul-infusion produces clear thinking, pure logic, and a living goal. The Soul-infused personality sees things as they really are. The mind becomes illumined and the divine Plan can be visualized. This creates group-consciousness, a sense of unity, synthesis and tolerance. A limitless horizon appears and deep aspiration towards the divine realities is created. The form cannot veil his vision. Man sees the motives and causes. The hidden storage of his Soul's knowledge becomes evident. He becomes aware of all past experiences of the Soul. When man learns to control his mind he can use it as a searchlight for deeper truths and as a creative agent for life in general. He starts to look beyond the mental field and experiences great expansions of consciousness, leading from the unreal to the real.

Soul-infusion means a gradual awakening to the purpose of Creation and ever-increasing awareness of the part the individual plays in the fulfillment of the divine purpose. Soul-infusion not only gives this prospect; it generates in man an inner urge to participate in the cosmic purpose by doing his share according to the level of his achievement. Soul-infusion provides man with endurance and enthusiasm to continue his high-level activities of light, despite difficulties, obstacles and trials. Nothing can stop his unfoldment and service. He feels a fountain of inspiration and courage within him which changes all his obstacles and problems into creative urges. From this moment on man starts to walk as a disciple of the great principles. He is aware that he has a guide, the Solar Angel; also he is aware that he is living, feeling and thinking in the light of that Presence according to the Plan. This he sees in the eyes of the age-long Presence. He has become a liberated man.

CHAPTER 17

THE LEVELS OF MAN

*People often do not know for a long time what goes on in the house of a neighbor.
Still longer remains unknown what is happening in another country. Therefore
it is not astonishing that, that which takes place on another plane is unknown.* [1]

—M. M.

Each will read into the words his own state of consciousness. [2]

—The Tibetan

We have no specific measure by which to gauge the levels of man, but we do
have measures which can give us an idea of where a man stands. Suppose a nuclear
physicist gives a public lecture about the atom, radiations and light. In the audience are many interested people: scientists, college students, politicians, artists
and laymen, and a few individuals who happened by. Picture this situation on a
graph numbering 100 to 2. Number 100 is the man who gives the lecture. He
knows his subject thoroughly and understands the scientific terms which he uses.
He speaks from his knowledge plus experience—these two words are very important. Now let's place various people from the audience on levels 85, 75, 60, 50, 40,
10, and 2. These numbers symbolize their ability to understand and the sum total
of their knowledge and experience—their levels. The lecturer will speak on level
100, but the next level man will understand him only 85 percent. The following
man will understand 75 percent and so on. After the lecture a 65-percent-level man
will ask a man on level two if he had enjoyed the lecture and the level-two man will
answer, "nonsense." These levels may be compared to the levels on which men
live.

Now let us imagine a man of high spiritual achievement. Suppose we have the
returned Christ giving a lecture. The same thing will happen as in olden days; the
level-two men will crucify Him. In olden days the words Christ spoke came from
the depth of His experience, from His wisdom and understanding. He was speaking
from His level of achievement and people were listening to Him from their level of
achievement, from their level of knowledge and experience. He was an ocean and
people were understanding in accordance with their tiny vessels of being.

From the appearance of Christ to the present, all true Christian activities are
nothing but a striving to gradually approach the source of the teaching. It is a
continuous but very slow change of levels. Century after century people are raising
their levels little by little towards that Light, the Christ, Who gave the teaching on
His own level. A huge procession is coming towards Him. There are those who are
coming closer to Him and those who are working very hard to follow His footsteps
through the hills and the valleys. The whole process is the changing of the levels.

Our understanding is the result of our knowledge, experience and wisdom. We

---

1. Agni Yoga Society, *Fiery World*, vol. 3, p. 377.
2. A. A. Bailey, *A Treatise on White Magic*, p. 24.

may know by heart the words of Christ but if we do not live by them, we cannot experience them. Hence we cannot understand the words, and our level does not change. All the misunderstanding of life is due to differences in the levels. We think and feel on one level and act on another. We speak on this level and listen on another. We love on one level but marry on a different level. We speak on this level and get angry when the answer comes from another level. Higher-level people love and sacrifice while lower-level people hate and persecute them.

In our daily life we see these levels at work. Take for example a teenager who smokes, stays out with members of the opposite sex until midnight, and uses alcohol. A high-level relative approaches him and says; "Look here. You are wasting energies which you can use in building your future." The teenager then goes to his nice mother and says: "Ma, I hate Uncle Joe. You know why? Because he wants to limit my freedom. I want to be free to do as I please so long as I am not hurting anybody. Freedom is our privilege. He can't force his ideas upon me. He can't force me to do things his way. I want to be free."

His mother's answer completely confuses the boy. "Son," she says, "he does not want you to be his slave; he wants you to use your mind to better advantage, and cease being the slave of your habits of smoking, using alcohol, etc. As long as you cannot control these habits you are their slave. Uncle Joe wants you to be set free." But our teenager shakes his head and goes away because he can understand these words only on his own level.

Not only do people live on different levels but each man has different levels within his being and life, upon which he descends or ascends. Take as example the lady who says to her teacher; "My level is declining these days. The level of my life, of my thinking and feeling is going down." "Why do you say this?" asks the teacher. "Don't you realize that to know yourself better is itself progress in being? Suppose you live in a room containing twelve mirrors, each mirror showing one aspect of your being. Here you have a great opportunity to face yourself as you are, on different occasions and under different conditions. You see yourself in many ways and this process of facing yourself is the process of knowing yourself. Each step taken toward self-knowledge is a step of progress in being, an achievement.

"In this case the important thing is not what you are. The important thing is the fact of seeing and observing yourself. The more you observe yourself, the more you detach your real self from what you are at that moment in time and space. The real self is the observer. The moment you identify yourself with your different activities, emotions or thoughts you lose yourself in them and your level goes down accordingly."

Here the most important thing to know is that it does not matter what you are or where you are at any given time, but how much and how far you can observe the little self. This is the basis of detachment, and progress. A guilt complex develops when you identify yourself with the activities of your body, emotions and mind. When you detach yourself from these activities and observe them, you have in your hand the best source of knowledge and experience, and are on the path to self-knowledge and liberation.

Every book we read, every word to which we listen is translated on our own level. If we are living upon a level higher than the book we are reading, we either find more in it than the author intended or we disregard it.

Some high-level books are written in such a way that they can draw many people from different levels, and give to each of them some guidance. But when these people do not begin to change their own level of being, they become enemies of that teaching because they create barriers upon the path of progress of other people.

The existence of the levels teaches us the importance of tolerance, open-mindedness, freedom of thought and a deep aspiration to be ready to accept truths. These are the basic keys which will open for us the door of the next level. Time is progress. Those who do not raise their level disintegrate.

Sometimes these levels are judged by outer appearances. We may say, this man is a high-level man. Why? Because he has a few million dollars and lives like a traditional king. Or we may say, those people have attained high positions in our society. But the levels which we are discussing have nothing to do with outer appearances. They are related to our inner achievement, or inner being and realization.

Many times the outer level of a man declines. For example a governor later becomes president of a big business, or an independent writer, or a leader of an organization. This does not mean that his inner level is lowered; sometimes quite the contrary is true. A classic example is the case of Socrates and his enemies, or Jesus and Judas. On the outer level Socrates and Jesus were defeated in the end, and their enemies were victorious, but on the inner scale Socrates and Jesus were the winners. Their teachings and spirit created civilizations and culture which are still extant today, and will continue into the future. Often an outer success is a defeat for our inner level, our inner man; and a seeming defeat is a great success or advancement on the inner level. If we study the past, we will see that all our most difficult lessons were learned at a time of crisis, difficulty or trouble, when our outer level was in danger or undergoing defeat.

How can we raise the level of our being? Only by conscious action and voluntary service. Conscious action *means* that all our activities on the three levels, physical, emotional and mental, must be controlled by ourselves. They must cease to have mechanical reactions and automatic responses. The *achievement* requires a conscious struggle within ourselves to change the level of our being through observation, detachment and *striving.* But this is not enough. We must then express our *new level of achievement* in our life through *greater* service and sacrifice. To serve is to radiate our inner achievement towards life. To serve means to build bridges in people and for people, enabling them to reach the stage where they can take destiny into their own hands. Through service we raise our level, because we cannot serve if we are not in continuous relation with higher levels. The streams of higher energies passing through us, as acts of service, purify us and prepare us for the next step. Only through service can we recognize our level and our need, and aspire to the higher worlds. Only through service does the transmutation of our inner world take place. Service is the practical technique of sublimation and transfiguration.

In a life of service we recognize that man, in order to hasten his development, must suffer. This suffering is voluntary and conscious, and is the fire in which the transmutation process takes place. Let us take the case of a man who is under attack by ignorant people, or of a cause which is going to be lost unless we take some action. We know what it will cost us: sleepless nights, continuous work, criticism, attack and more. Nevertheless we enter the fight because we see that it is worth protecting something existing on a higher level; and by protecting, fighting and suffering we raise our level through these experiences.

We can only attain to love, purity, power and wisdom if they have been earned in our daily life of service and sacrifice. We cannot achieve higher qualities unless we earn them in the fire of our aspirations and struggles. We have no purity unless we acquire it by passing through tests. Wisdom can only be attained when we act intelligently in the solving of all our problems and difficulties. Love, purity, power and wisdom do not belong to us unless they become a part of our being, and we are living by them, in them and through them. Gradual approach to the inner man or to the higher principles of the life means progress, or changing our level of being. Our higher level of being is not something given to us; it is gained through living a conscious life, for it is a level of understanding, the level of our love and wisdom. No one can reach a higher level by reading books, but rather by living his visions, loves, ideas and purposes. Only through an act of sacrifice can one realize the meaning of sacrifice. Until you have loved someone or something you cannot know what love really is, and then your love is only equal to the sacrifice you make for it.

Most people are born upon a certain level and fluctuate within that level throughout their lives. Many people advance a few levels and then lose the vision. Others retrogress from their level and degenerate. But we cannot remain long on any level because nothing can prevent advancement. To stop means to descend, because all life naturally goes forward. Those who progress enter into the "life more abundant," while those who come to a standstill become fuel for the cars of the people who go forward, upward.

There is no place in life or on the way of achievement where one can stop and say, "*I achieved,*" for at that very moment you are ejected from the path of progress.

Let us transfigure our being in our daily life, gradually passing step by step towards *our divine destiny.*

CHAPTER 18

SOUL CONSCIOUSNESS AND ITS SOCIAL EFFECTS

My warriors, guard thyselves with the shield of God's will, and the Divine Song will ever find echo within thee. Before the deluge, when men were wedding and feasting and bargaining, Noah was already selecting the most stalwart oaks for his Ark.[1]

—M. M.

Once a man recognizes himself as a soul, and affirms that he is a soul, an immense change takes place in his life. A great flood of Light pours into his mind and clears up the agelong obstacles, illusions and thought-forms that have kept him a slave of his past.

The first effect of this change is that energy accumulates in him. Because he does not misuse it, he no longer has any leakage due to wrong thinking and negative emotions, and therefore continuously receives precipitation of energy. Such a man has become a fountain of power which heals, uplifts and leads.

The second effect of the change is that the man becomes an agent of liberation in his social and national environment. He works to liberate the human soul from all inertia, glamors and illusions which are making our planet a place of sorrow, slavery, racial discrimination, fear, prejudice and selfishness. This task will put tremendous pressure on his vehicles and cause him much suffering...and joy.

The third effect of soul-consciousness will be the creation of simplicity in living and sincerity of expression.

The fourth effect will be a dynamic sense of communication and right human relations. We cannot create right human relations until a large percentage of humanity becomes soul-conscious and realizes the supreme meaning of the words;

> "The sons of men are one
> and I am one with them."

The fifth effect will be transmutation of a person into a magnetic and radio-active Personality, which automatically will group people around him to serve the cause of human liberation. The universal or global revolution has not started yet. Greater revolutionists will gradually appear in all the fields of human endeavor and, this time, they will inflame the hearts and souls of all true humanitarians throughout the world who will be charged with the spirit of greater dedication, aspiration and sacrifice. These leaders, having achieved soul-consciousness, will not stop at any obstacle and, through stupendous self-sacrifice, will lead humanity

---

1. Agni Yoga Society, *Leaves of Morya's Garden,* p. 37.

as a whole towards a higher dimension of living, the introduction of which is set forth in part, in the Universal Declaration of Human Rights and in the United Nations Charter.

Throughout the ages, opponents of progress for humanity and its unfoldment have opposed the universal liberation of mankind, the concept of Soul, of Immortality, and man's transformation into divinity. Soul-consciousness will end all religious, political and financial exploitation, thus leading humanity progressively forward. The coming revolution can be kept on the mental level, without tears or bloodshed, if the greater percentage of humanity responds to the Rays of the New Age and synchronizes all its life expressions with them. If the greater part of humanity does not respond to the keynote of the New Age, however, and if the political, economic and social conditions continue as they are at present, then the leaders of the New Age, the Soul-conscious people, and all people who are dedicated to the liberation of humanity will arise and the revolution of the planet will commence. This will be a revolution for the liberation of all humanity and will be the most crucial revolution in the history of the planet.

To the degree that a man approaches his Soul and becomes a *Soul* does he become an independent human being and a being of greater cooperation. Many people think that independence is conditioned by outer events, but in reality it starts from within. Man cannot be independent unless he breaks all the inner chains, the inner slavery and the inner imprisonment. Once freed from inertia, glamors and illusions, he enters the freedom of his soul consciousness and becomes an independent, self-activated, and self-determined man. Before this inner freedom has been achieved, his outer freedom contributes only to his own destruction and suffering.

Education and knowledge often lead man to group or national independence, to attacks and wars. Soul-consciousness does not work for personal, group or national freedom alone; it works for the planetary and global independence and leads to an everlasting sense of unity, because the Soul is group conscious and stands for all humanity and its highest good.

When people who stand above racial discrimination, religious separation, dogmas and doctrines, increase on the planet, they will recognize one another and will hold each other's hands from east to west and from north to south. Then a new dawn will break upon humanity and "the orphan of the Planet," mankind itself, will experience a great release of joy which had been imprisoned within man for ages and ages due to human slavery and ignorance. This will be the age of health, trust, joy, understanding and cooperation.

The sixth effect of soul-consciousness will be the elimination of the fear of death and the acquisition of a continuous radiation of sacrifice for one's fellow man.

The seventh effect will be a universal sense of harmlessness and a deep, fiery devotion to the flame of life in every form, from the flower on the earth to the stars in the firmament.

Then, my dear one, the vision of St. John will come true;

"And I saw a new heaven and a new earth; for the first heaven and the first earth had passed away and the sea was no more....and He shall wipe away all tears from their eyes; and there shall be no more death, neither sorrow nor wailing, neither shall there be any more pain..."

OM MANI PADME
HUM